ANCIENT WISDOM FOR MODERN LIVING

For all the wisdom keepers,
and in loving memory of Sarah Dening

An Hachette UK Company
www.hachette.co.uk

First published in Great Britain in 2019 by
Kyle Books, an imprint of Kyle Cathie Ltd
Carmelite House
50 Victoria Embankment
London EC4Y 0DZ
www.kylebooks.co.uk

ISBN: 978 085783 704 2

Designer: *Cathy McKinnon*
Illustrator: *Maggie Cole*
Project Editor: *Sophie Allen*
Editorial Assistant: *Sarah Kyle*
Production: *Caroline Alberti*

A Cataloguing in Publication record for this title is available
from the British Library.

Printed and bound in China

10 9 8 7 6 5 4 3 2 1

DISCLAIMER: The authors and publishers do not accept any responsibility
for loss, harm or damage from the use or misuse of this book, or your failure
to seek proper medical advice.

ANCIENT WISDOM FOR MODERN LIVING

From Ayurveda to Zen,
Seasonal Wisdom for Clarity and Balance

JANE ALEXANDER

ILLUSTRATIONS BY MAGGIE COLE

KYLE BOOKS

CONTENTS

LATE SUMMER

AUTUMN

WINTER

INTRODUCTION

The ancients knew a thing or two, they really did. Modern science is only just catching up with concepts our ancestors understood millennia ago. Ayurveda, the medicine of ancient India, had detailed knowledge of paediatrics and psychiatry, surgery and toxicology 3,000 years ago. Over 2,500 years ago, the Greek sage, Hippocrates, claimed that we should be aiming for a healthy mind in a healthy body, yet the interplay of mental, emotional and physical health is only just being accepted by modern doctors.

An understanding of the quantum realm permeates the sacred texts of India and Tibet, as well as the Qabalah, the esoteric side of Judaism. The great quantum physicists Bohr, Heisenberg and Schrödinger read the Vedas (Indian sacred texts) and were inspired by ancient Indian and Chinese thought. And those are just the cultures that wrote down their wisdom – many others, equally ancient and learned, kept to an oral tradition. So, this book is the very antithesis of a new fad. This is living wisdom that has been used for thousands

of years. It has been tried and tested by literally millions of people, handed down from generation to generation for one simple reason: it works.

I have been studying this cornucopia of wisdom for the last 30 years. I was lucky enough, first as a journalist and then as an author, to interview countless wisdom keepers in the ancient traditions. In this book, I'll be introducing you to techniques from a wide variety of sources. However, the main focus will fall on the great healing traditions of Traditional Chinese Medicine (TCM), Ayurveda and

Tibetan medicine – purely because these are the ones of which I have the most experience. Sadly, European wisdom traditions were not able to develop and flourish in the same way – mainly because so many of our wise women and men (the so-called witches) were murdered in the burning times. However, a diluted form has survived in naturopathy so we'll certainly be diving into some of these cures. Equally, many of the great healing traditions of the Americas, Africa and Australia were decimated by colonialism – it's heartrending to think how much knowledge has been killed along with its guardians.

Ancient wisdom sees health as something far more than simple lack of disease – it is living at one's fullest. It is an integration of mind, body and those ineffable concepts of soul and spirit. It is about connection – with ourselves, with our community and with the wider world.

So I also call on the shamanic traditions that shaped our ancestors' worlds, with their understanding of our inescapable link with nature – we are human animals, not separate and not so special. Modern psychology is now realising things that were common knowledge in the old world – we need a connection with nature, with our planet. We are social animals – we need community, we need ritual, we need meaning. Our ancestors knew this. They came together to celebrate the yearly cycle of the seasons, the life passages of the tribe. They gathered around the fire and told stories, shared hopes and fears, supported one another in joy and grief. Nowadays we often live in separation, each tucked away in our little boxes – we yearn for the ancient hearth, for communal warmth, for the widest sense of family. We are not meant to be alone. So we won't just look at healing our bodies – we will spread our net wide.

I have designed this book so you can dip in and out. The hope is that you will feel inspired to try just a few new ideas, to make little tweaks to your lifestyle. Be warned, this kind of authentic living is addictive and you may well find your new habits snowballing into a new way of living – a good one, I hasten to add.

I have split the content into the seasons. Our forebears watched the natural world. They learned that every season possesses a different energy and that, if we want to stay healthy and happy, we need to adapt our lives according to the wheel of the year. This thinking lies at the heart of Ayurveda, Tibetan medicine, Chinese Five Element medicine and the indigenous American traditions – to name just a few. It makes sense that we should shift and adapt our diet and lifestyle according to the season. Despite all our advances, all our technology, we are still governed by the rhythms of the natural world. Nature has cycles – times of thrusting vitality, relaxed plenty, storing and harvesting and times for withdrawal and rest. In the past, we had little choice but to follow the shifting pattern of the year. Our ancestors lived close to the land; they knew its cycles like the backs of their hands. Yet we no longer watch the sky, the earth, the rivers and seas – we have fallen out of communion with our wider world. If nothing else, I'd love it if you could be more aware of your relationship with this still beautiful world in which we live.

Let's start with some basic background on the forms of healing we'll be investigating. Please be aware that this book is merely scratching the surface of the fountain of ancient wisdom. My hope is that *Ancient Wisdom for Modern Living* might inspire you to delve deeper, to find a tradition that inspires you, that calls to you, and to explore with your heart wide open.

THE
ANCIENT
WISDOMS

AYURVEDA

Ayurveda is known as the 'Mother of Medicine'. At least 5,000 years old, the ancient Indian texts call it 'eternal' as its principles were said to have been passed down to humankind from a chain of gods leading back to Brahma, father of all gods. The name comes from two Sanskrit words – 'ayus', meaning life, and 'veda' meaning knowledge.

We are so lucky that written texts document the tenets and history of Ayurveda. They suggest that the medicine practised from about 1,500 BCE to 500 CE was incredibly advanced, with detailed knowledge of paediatrics, psychiatry, surgery, geriatrics, toxicology, general medicine and other specialities. Students studied six philosophical systems: the study of logic; evolution and causality; the discipline of body and spirit (yoga); moral behaviour; pure esoteric knowledge; and even the theory of the atom.

When India suffered invasions in the Middle Ages, the system began to fall apart and the universities were broken up. The British were the final nail in the coffin of Ayurveda, bringing Western medicine with them from the eighteenth century, and establishing their own universities. Luckily, the Indian Congress affirmed support for Ayurveda in 1921 when Mahatma Gandhi opened the first new college for Ayurvedic medicine. Now Ayurveda is routinely practised alongside Western medicine in India.

Ayurvedic physicians undergo vigorous medical training for five or six years. Full-on Ayurveda can be stringent, to put it mildly. Daily schedules could involve rising before sunrise for a routine involving tongue scraping, body oiling, yoga, meditation – all before breakfast. Some parts of Ayurveda may appear a tad flaky. Physicians may prescribe particular types of jewellery or colours of clothing but, as we'll see, there is method in their apparent madness – colours do affect us, both physically and emotionally, while crystals carry particular healing frequencies.

Personally, I find a full-on Ayurvedic lifestyle simply too tough to fit in with a modern Western lifestyle. It can get very complicated. However, I do think it's really worth looking into to understand your fundamental nature and how you might be falling out of balance. There are some really simple fixes and tweaks that can make a lot of difference.

PHILOSOPHY

Body and mind are seen as inseparable in Ayurveda; each influences the other. Then there is 'soul' – an eternal form of energy which is said to animate our mind–body. Each person's individual soul-energy is, in turn, linked with the wider energies of the universal soul and cosmic energy. So we are separate yet part of the whole, linked with other people and allied with the universe. I find this a hugely comforting thought.

It also has a knock-on effect in daily life. It's not enough to make changes purely on the physiological level – health and wellbeing come about by achieving harmony both within ourselves and within our wider environment. If we could all take that on board, wouldn't our world be a different place?

The Ayurvedic texts teach that beyond the cosmos lies a state of pure consciousness that developed a desire to experience itself. This led to a split into primordial universal energy (purusa) and cosmic substance (prakruti). Purusa is active and energising; it breathes life into prakruti, bringing about three essential qualities known as the gunas – sattva, rajas and tamas. Sattva consists of truth, beauty and equilibrium; rajas is all about power and impetus; while tamas manifests as restriction and obstruction.

From tamas rise the elements – ether, air, fire, water and earth – from which the physical world around us is born.

Each physical atom consists of the five elements: its weight comes from earth, its cohesion from water, its energy from fire, its motion from air and the space between its particles are made of ether. So the whole human body is composed of the five elements and an excess or lack of one or more elements can be the cause of imbalance, eventually leading to illness.

DOSHAS AND DIAGNOSIS

Over time, Ayurveda came up with a form of shorthand for working out imbalances – three bioenergies or doshas, which are combinations of the five elements. Vata is a combination of ether and air; pitta of fire with water; kapha of water and earth. In an ideal state, we would have all three doshas in perfect balance. Unsurprisingly, this is rare.

The dosha that dominates within our body gives rise to our prakruti, or mind–body type. This affects everything about us – our shape and weight, our predisposition to certain illnesses, the kinds of food we should eat, how we react to situations.

Finding and balancing your doshas can be a truly liberating experience. People who have never been able to lose weight can find the excess simply vanishing as they rid their body of the foods that increase kapha. Equally, those who are just 'too spacey' can find a vata-soothing lifestyle will bring them down to earth. The benefits aren't just physical: soothing imbalanced doshas can help your memory and concentration, can allow you to sleep better, help you deal with stress, anxiety and depression, make you less irritable and even improve your sex life.

Where Ayurveda can become confusing is when you find that, although you are predominantly, say, vata, you also seem to have several strong characteristics of another dosha that seem to contradict your main one. In an ideal world, I'd say consult an Ayurvedic physician for an individualised programme. However, you can go a long way working with common sense and intuition. **Let's look at the three doshas for an overview.**

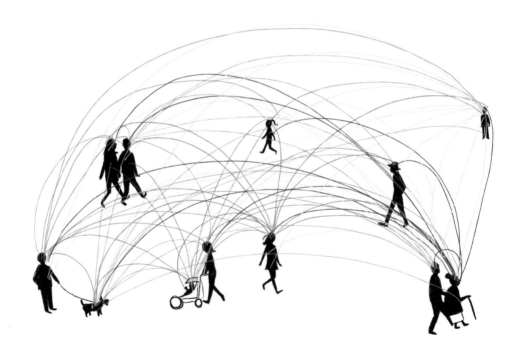

Vata (air and ether)

Physical characteristics: Slim with light bones, prominent joints and tendons. Rarely puts on weight. Skin is dry and delicate, easily affected by the weather. Hands are usually cold with little perspiration. Nails are often brittle. Appetite is irregular – sometimes ravenous, sometimes can't be bothered. Loves to snack or nibble. Walks quickly and always seems to be in a hurry.

Mind and emotions: Enthusiastic, outgoing and talkative, but with changeable moods and thoughts. Highly creative, imaginative and full of ideas; quickly becomes bored with routine. Easily becomes stressed and anxious. Dreams frequently but can't remember dreams on waking.

When vata is unbalanced: Can cause constipation, bloating and wind, aching joints, dry skin and hair, brittle nails, headaches, sharp pains, eczema or dry rashes, nervous disorders, failing memory, confusion.

Times dominated by vata energy: 2–6pm and 2–6am. Vata seasons are autumn and winter.

Diet: The vata-soothing diet is all about warm, unctuous comfort food – think bowls of pasta drenched in sauce, porridge, cosy apple crumbles. A certain amount of natural sweetness and oiliness (sweet fruit, butter, oil, maple syrup) is good. Avoid cold foods and iced drinks, dry or frozen foods or leftovers. Raw food and juices are a big no-no for vata too.

Exercise: Vata's natural inclination is for fast high-energy sports and activities – running (sprinting in particular), HIIT, spinning, downhill skiing, fast-paced classes with loud music. To soothe vata, slow the pace – hill walking (taking in the view, rather than focusing on the Fitbit), yoga, Pilates or tai chi are ideal.

Lifestyle: Regularity and routine are key. Learn to recognise the signs of overdrive and slow down. Meditation is vata's best friend. Calm, gentle creative pursuits will soothe vata beautifully. Keeping warm (in all senses) is vital – a safe, caring environment, with steams and saunas. Hygge, and its Scottish cousin, coorie, are made for vata. Getting enough sleep will also help to keep vata on an even keel – avoid late nights and night shifts.

Pitta (fire and water)

Physical characteristics: Average build and bone structure. Can easily gain and lose weight. Skin is soft and may tend to be reddish or freckled. Hands often perspire a lot. Nails are flexible but quite strong. Appetite is good. Irritable if forced to skip meals. Loves high-protein foods. Pitta walks purposefully and in a determined fashion.

Mind and emotions: Strong-minded and purposeful, thrives on challenges and is a natural leader with a keen intellect. Efficient and perfectionist (can be a bit bossy), likes well-planned routines. Becomes angry or irritable under stress. Dreams vividly and often in colour – easily remembers dreams.

When pitta is unbalanced: Can cause rashes and allergies, inflammation, heartburn, ulcers, acidity, feverish complaints, sore throats, intense feelings of anger, frustration or jealousy.

Times dominated by pitta energy: 10am–2pm and 10pm–2am. Pitta season is high summer.

Diet: Pitta usually loves hot spicy foods, meat and alcohol (they're the typical curry and beer, or steak and red wine types). Unfortunately, this diet doesn't love them back. Cut right down on greasy foods, caffeine, salt, red meat, alcohol and highly spiced foods to soothe pitta. Cooling calming foods – fresh fruit and vegetables, milk, soft cheeses, wholegrains and bitter greens – may sound boring but they balance pitta a treat.

Exercise: Pitta adores any form of competitive sport – even a simple game of ping-pong brings out the killer instinct. Solo workouts can teach pitta to focus on how they are feeling, rather than watching everyone else. Slow focused forms of yoga (yin or hatha rather than ashtanga) are superb. Water sports are supremely calming and soothing for pitta while winter sports in the snow and ice also help cool the pitta fire.

Lifestyle: Keeping cool (in all ways) is the key to balancing pitta. Avoiding physical heat, staying out of the sun and steering clear of steams and saunas will help, as will steering clear of emotional and intellectual conflicts. A cool shower or bath is ideal or, at the least, finish off with a cool rinse. Pitta is highly organised so introducing some spontaneity stops life becoming too goal-orientated. Take a walk or muse out of the window 'just for the hell of it'. Doing absolutely nothing is highly therapeutic (if painful) for pitta.

Kapha (earth and water)

Physical characteristics: Large boned and heavy build with broad shoulders and wide hips. Finds it hard to lose weight. Skin can be oily, but is usually cool to the touch. Nails are thick and strong, and hair can be oily. Enjoys food and doesn't like skipping meals (but can easily do so without ill effects). Loves fatty, starchy foods. Walks slowly and steadily.

Mind and emotions: Easy-going, reliable, and calm. Thrives on a regular routine, keeps projects running smoothly and steadily. A great team player. Will avoid stress at all costs. Only remembers very clear or significant dreams.

When kapha is unbalanced: Can become prone to excess weight, fluid retention, excess mucus, bronchitis, sinus problems, asthma, congestion, frequent colds, depression.

Times dominated by kapha energy:
6–10am and 6–10pm. Kapha season
is spring.

Diet: Kapha needs to say no to iced food
and drinks, cut right down on sugar, and
avoid too much bread (gluten is often a
problem). Dairy can also aggravate kapha,
producing mucus. Light, warm and dry
foods suit kapha – nothing too stodgy or
greasy. A certain amount of carbohydrate
is fine – light grains such as millet, barley
or rye work well – and plenty of fresh
vegetables are healing. Sprinkle herbs
and spices liberally. Kapha could also do
with watching portion size – a smaller
plate could ease off that tendency to
gain weight.

Exercise: Kapha will happily lounge
around doing nothing – although their
strength and stamina make them great
at endurance sports and most shot

putters and wrestlers have kapha in their
makeup. Challenge kapha with activities
that stimulate both mind and body –
Zumba, kickboxing, martial arts. Kapha
needs plenty of physical exercise – try to
incorporate activity into every day.

Lifestyle: Kapha feels safe and snug when
everything stays the same so shaking
things up a little can stop life becoming
sluggish. Simple things like varying the
route to work or shifting round the living
room can help. Watch different types
of movies or TV shows. Check out new
evening classes or meetups to learn new
things and meet different people. Letting
go is also key. Kapha hoards, clinging
onto things like grim death – be it people,
emotions, physical weight.

TRADITIONAL CHINESE MEDICINE
(TCM)

In ancient China, you paid your doctor while you were well and stopped paying when you became sick. It was, and still is, the ultimate form of preventative medicine.

Patients were taught how to eat correctly, how to exercise, how to breathe, and how to adjust their home and work environment for optimum living. Tonics were given to ease the change into each season, to keep in perfect balance with the world around us. If you did fall sick, you would be given acupuncture, acupressure, herbal remedies or particular forms of bodywork.

Nowadays, more and more strands of ancient Chinese culture are becoming accepted. Research is ongoing into acupuncture and Chinese herbalism. Massage therapists are learning techniques such as acupressure and tuina and finding their clients respond with amazing results. Feng shui, the Chinese art of placement in architecture and interior design, is becoming accepted even by hard-nosed businesspeople. Even the complex oracle, the I Ching, is being used increasingly as a tool for greater happiness and success, teaching people the best and most auspicious time and way to proceed in important life choices.

To the Chinese it all seems very obvious. All of life is energy and energy is constantly changing and flowing. The energy that abounds with the bright morning sun is quite different from that of the glowing sunset; the vigorous thrusting energy of spring cannot be compared to the apparent emptiness of winter; a cluttered apartment has a completely different atmosphere from a soaring cathedral. In order to pass through life healthily and successfully you need to get into the flow, to move seamlessly in harmony with the vital energies of the earth and cosmos, rather than fighting against them.

The underlying philosophy is that good health (in body, mind and spirit) revolves around the correct flow of 'qi' (pronounced 'chi'), the subtle energy of the body. Qi flows around the body in channels called meridians; along the meridians lie hundreds of points that link the various organs and functions of the body. Ayurveda has the same concept – it calls vital energy, prana, and the acupoints are described as 'marma' points.

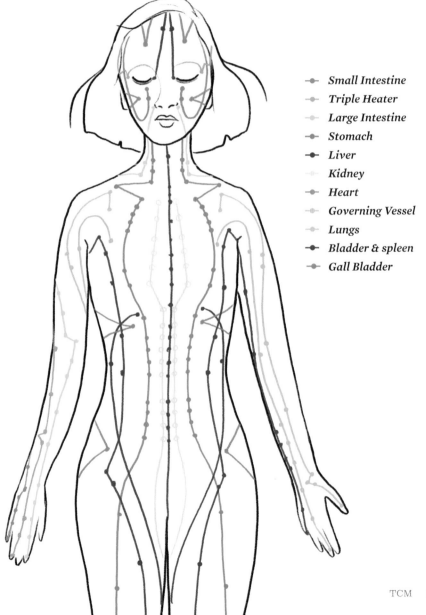

- Small Intestine
- Triple Heater
- Large Intestine
- Stomach
- Liver
- Kidney
- Heart
- Governing Vessel
- Lungs
- Bladder & spleen
- Gall Bladder

If we look after ourselves, eating the right kinds of food, doing the right kinds of exercise, keeping our bodies and minds balanced, the qi in our bodies will flow smoothly and correctly. If we make unhealthy lifestyle choices, our levels of qi fall out of balance with a corresponding drop in vital energy or even the possibility of disease. In a similar way, qi flows through houses and landscapes and can be blocked or allowed to rush through in a completely undisciplined manner.

YIN AND YANG

According to TCM, the world is also divided into two forces – yin and yang. Yin is considered to be mysterious, unrevealed, hidden, esoteric. It's the energy of contraction, of gathering energy, the hibernating potential. Meanwhile yang is expansive, outward moving, rising activity, expending energy. It's the expression of potential. Each has the seed of the other within it because all is movement and flow. When we're in balance our energy moves constantly between the two poles. The well-known symbol is a fabulous sign of eternal flow.

In addition, there are the five elements to consider: fire, earth, metal (or air), water and wood. When TCM practitioners diagnose, they don't just check for the flow of qi, they are looking to see how much of each element is within the body and what kind of energy is being transmitted. Then they can stimulate or quieten unbalanced organs or body systems by food, exercise, massage, herbs or the needles of acupuncture.

While Western science is just beginning to accept the idea of biorhythms, natural shifts in human energy, the Chinese have known about it for thousands of years. They divide each day into different phases according to the kind of energy that prevails – yang rules from midnight until noon while yin moves in to govern noon until midnight. Recognising that human energy shifts accordingly, early morning has always been associated for the Chinese with high energy while mid-afternoon (high yin time) is yawning siesta time. Orthodox physiologists are now discovering what the Chinese have always known: each organ receives energy at different times of the day or year. Asthma attacks don't occur more frequently in the night by chance, but because 3am is the time when the lungs are at the height of their energetic activity. High noon is the most likely time to have a heart attack because this is the hour of the heart's maximum activity. Why do most people have their major bowel movement first thing in the morning? You could put it down to potty training, but more likely it's because the large intestine receives the largest amount of energy at that time.

Yin and yang work in larger cycles too. Each month has its yin and yang phases – yin rules from the full moon until the new moon, while yang takes over from the new moon until the moon is full once again. And the whole year shifts to the yin/yang rhythm – fresh new yang rises with bounding energy and vitality in spring and reaches its full, abundant maturity in the height of summer. Then yin begins to rise and takes us down through the quiet of autumn into the depths of winter.

THE 'EVIL' ENERGIES

We all carry all the various elements within us and, in an ideal world, they would all be in balance. However, perhaps inevitably given the stress, strain and pollution of modern life, few of us are naturally in balance. Poor food choices, insufficient exercise and the numerous environmental pollutants in the world take their toll. Our bodies don't naturally adapt to the shifts in energy that occur with each season and so we fall ill or feel generally under par. The Chinese would say that we have fallen prey to an 'evil' energy, upsetting the delicate internal balance between yin and yang.

THE FIVE ELEMENTS

Wood

The element associated with spring, wood is the fresh yang stage of the seasonal cycle – young, expansive, energetic and explosive. It provides creative energy, increased sexuality, vigour and growth. Wood energy within the body nourishes the muscles and the tissues. It governs the gall bladder and the liver. Within the psyche it calls for free expression, for the freedom and space to explore ideas, to try new things. If wood is blocked it can cause feelings of frustration, stagnation, jealousy and anger.

Fire

This is the element of summer, which arises when the creative power of wood grows and matures into the full yang of fire. This is the creative force at the height of its power – everything is expansive, fully grown, satisfied. Fire, quite naturally, warms the heart and human emotions. Within the body it circulates the blood and keeps our own vital energy, or qi, moving. It is also responsible for the digestive fire of the small intestine. Fire is open and generous, abundant, joyous and brave. If you block fire it can cause heart problems, hypertension or disorders of the nervous system, giving us a tendency to become nervous, hysterical or neurotic.

Earth

A strange time – although the Chinese divide the year neatly into four seasons they also recognise a fifth, a period between high summer and autumn in which everything is in perfect balance. It is a mellow time during which neither yin nor yang rule. This is the fulcrum of the year – everything is poised, everything is full and ripe; it provides a feeling of ease and well-being, comfort and completeness. Earth is the embodiment of nourishment and vitality and governs the stomach so, not surprisingly, if earth becomes unbalanced or is deficient in your system you will find you have problems with digestion. When we are in balance, we easily digest and process both food and information.

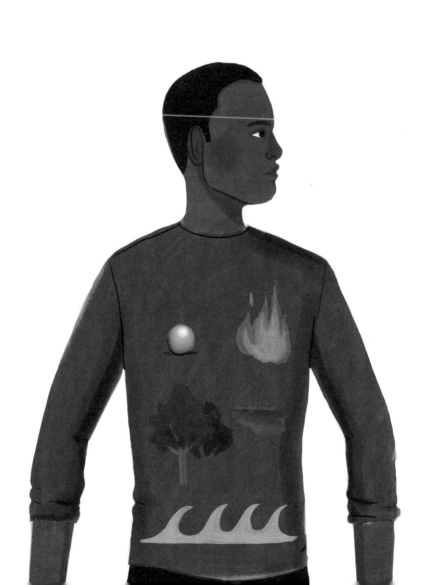

Metal

Energy is shifting into its yin phase as autumn arrives, contracting, condensing, beginning to store and save itself for the lean months ahead, just as in the fields the harvest has been brought in to feed humans and animals through the winter. It's a time for jettisoning the old and unnecessary, keeping only the healthy and vital to see us through the dark days ahead. In the body, metal controls the lungs and the large intestine. Blocked metal energy will produce chest infections, skin complaints, different strains of flu, colds and respiratory problems. On a psychological level, it will cause feelings of grief and sadness, melancholy and anxiety.

Water

Come winter, yin has moved into its most extreme state. Everything is still and cold, waiting and resting. Energy is being condensed, conserved, held in storage until the thrusting yang energy rises again. To the Chinese, water is considered a highly concentrated element whose power is potential, awaiting release, like a cat bunched and paused to spring. In our bodies, water rules over the fluids in our systems – the hormones, the mysterious lymph, the slow bone marrow, the essential enzymes. This is a time to store and to keep warm, a time to conserve vital energy and go deep within. If water becomes unbalanced it can cause chills and fevers, headaches and a variety of other bodily aches and pains. It can even cause sexual impotence.

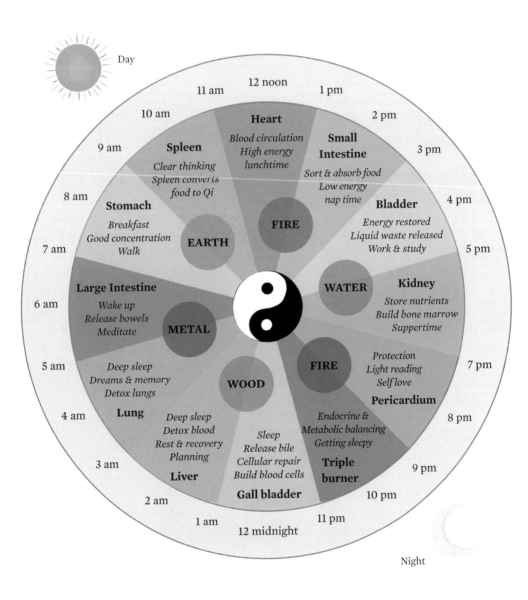

CHINESE MEDICINE
24-HOUR CIRCADIAN CLOCK

Day

12 noon
11 am   1 pm
10 am   2 pm
9 am   3 pm

Heart
Blood circulation
High energy
lunchtime

Spleen
Clear thinking
Spleen converts
food to Qi

Small
Intestine
Sort & absorb food
Low energy
nap time

FIRE

8 am   4 pm

Stomach
Breakfast
Good concentration
Walk

EARTH

Bladder
Energy restored
Liquid waste released
Work & study

7 am   5 pm

Large Intestine
Wake up
Release bowels
Meditate

METAL

WATER

Kidney
Store nutrients
Build bone marrow
Suppertime

6 am

Deep sleep
Dreams & memory
Detox lungs

WOOD

FIRE

Protection
Light reading
Self love

5 am   7 pm

Lung
Deep sleep
Detox blood
Rest & recovery
Planning

Sleep
Release bile
Cellular repair
Build blood cells

Pericardium

Endocrine &
Metabolic balancing
Getting sleepy

4 am   8 pm

Liver

Gall bladder

Triple
burner

3 am   9 pm

2 am   10 pm
1 am   11 pm
12 midnight

Night

TRADITIONAL TIBETAN MEDICINE

Tibetan medicine is ancient and venerable. It also appears to work – startlingly well. Reports have suggested that Tibetan physicians have cured 'incurable' diseases and many desperate people have flown thousands of miles to ask their opinions and to take their unique herbal preparations known as 'precious pills'. Yet the Tibetan tradition of healing has always remained rather arcane and unapproachable, simply because few Westerners had the basic tools (a working knowledge of modern and ancient Tibetan) to learn the system or the patience to complete the training (it takes at least ten years).

I was lucky enough to meet Kate Roddick over 20 years ago. Kate is one of the most knowledgeable people in the West when it comes to this ancient healing system.

Tibetans classify all of life into five energies which combine to create three 'humours' – air, bile and phlegm. There are clear similarities with Ayurveda, and Tibetan medicine has many crossover points with both Ayurveda and TCM.

Air controls breathing, speech and muscular activity, the nervous system, thought processes and your emotional attitude. Bile governs heat in the body, the liver and the digestive tract; while phlegm controls the amount of mucus in the body and also regulates the immune system. When all the humours are in balance you will enjoy perfect health. When one or more becomes aggravated or sluggish, problems will occur.

It sounds simple but Tibetan healing is so precise and complex that it can be mind-boggling: it takes a very experienced physician to bring about the kind of 'miracle' cures that occur. However, with just a little knowledge we could all make ourselves healthier.

Diet is very important and practitioners believe that often food is the only medicine required to obtain the necessary balance. It's a philosophy that is now being espoused by practitioners of functional or lifestyle medicine.

Expect careful questioning and pulse-taking (as with Chinese medicine, Tibetan healing checks a variety of pulses to gauge health). In addition, the Tibetans use urine diagnosis for precise information on the person (tested at the beginning of the day). The massage feels wonderful: it uses spiced or herbalised oils and works on the acupressure points to free blockages. Then you will be advised on diet and told which foods to avoid. Lifestyle tips may be given too. Herbs tend to be prescribed in the form of tiny pills.

WHAT'S YOUR TIBETAN TYPE?

Most people are a combination of types, but this should give you a rough idea of which humour is dominating at present.

Lung/air

Air causes stress. You might sweat very little and could suffer from insomnia, constipation, back pains, dry skin and stomach disorders. Your mind might flit from subject to subject. Symptoms include restlessness, dizziness, shivering, sighing, pain in hips and shoulder blades, humming in ears.
A clear sign of unbalanced air is watery, almost transparent, urine. Air equates to the vata dosha in Ayurveda.

Tripa/bile

Bile people often sweat quite a lot. They are precise, analytical people with good mental powers but can be a little antisocial. They often wake up feeling bright and cheerful but by midday are feeling irritable. Their weak spot is their liver and they can easily overheat. When bile is out of balance you could feel thirsty, have a bitter taste in your mouth, pains in the upper body, feel feverish and have diarrhoea or vomiting.
Unbalanced bile can be diagnosed if your urine is brownish in colour. Bile equates to pitta dosha in Ayurveda.

Pegan/phlegm

The phlegmatic person is generally heavy. They have even, stable and (sometimes) stubborn personalities and avoid rows. They are prone to over-sleeping and like an afternoon siesta. Their problems tend to be bronchial or in the kidneys. If phlegm is out of balance you could feel lethargic and heavy; have frequent indigestion or belching; distention of the stomach and a feeling of coldness in the feet. You might put on weight or find it hard to lose weight.
Disordered phlegm shows in very pale, foaming urine. Phlegm equates to kapha dosha in Ayurveda.

TIBB

Tibb (also known as Unani medicine, Sufi medicine or Greco-Arabic medicine) has been practised across vast areas of the world for thousands of years. Even today it is still the main source of medicine in large areas of India, Pakistan, Bangladesh, Afghanistan, Malaysia and the Middle East.

This ancient wisdom has incorporated knowledge from ancient Egyptian and Greek medicine, from the Chinese and Indian traditions and from the ancient healing wisdom of Persia and the Middle East.

At first sight, Tibb shares much with traditional Chinese, Tibetan or Ayurvedic medicine. Like these, Tibb recognises vital energy (known in Arabic as 'qawa'). It shares the concept that medicine needs to be holistic, to look at the whole person. It regards the correct balance of elements within the body as essential to health and it uses a battery of herbal remedies to combat modern ills. However, Tibb has unique strengths and qualities that make it worthy of a wider recognition.

Firstly Tibb is a very gentle medicine. Where Chinese and Tibetan doctors would treat first with diet, Tibb physicians look at lifestyle, at the most subtle levels. A physician would most likely start by adjusting our breathing – it's a small and subtle change that can have a huge effect.

Next they look at the emotions. In India, Pakistan and Bangladesh where Tibb is taught in universities, a major part of the hakim (practitioner) training involves counselling and psychotherapy. What we think and imagine can affect our health in a profound way.

Then they investigate your sleeping pattern, your eating regime, your bowel movements. They will study your working life and how you relax and try to find ways of making your life work for you in the most healthy yet realistic ways. Then, and only then, would they use herbs.

If you have a structural problem they might employ osteopathic manipulations or massage techniques. Finally, if they feel your problem has a deeper, spiritual basis, they would use what is known as logotherapy, finding ways that fit your belief system or religion to soothe your very soul. So Tibb is holistic in the true sense of the word – the physician is looking at every patient on four levels: the physical, the emotional, the intellectual and the spiritual, and treating accordingly. I find it possibly the most satisfying of all systems of health.

My consultation with a Tibb physician

was intriguing. It felt like talking to a doctor and a psychotherapist rolled into one. As with the Chinese, Ayurvedic and Tibetan systems, Tibb relies on the pulses for diagnosis. The physician also looks at body shape, complexion, eyes, tongue and our whole manner to decide on one's basic constitution or 'mijaz'. The whole experience feels like a wonderful mixture of the clinical and the nurturing.

Tibb does not tend to treat accident or emergency cases, or anyone who needs an operation (although they can often avert the need for surgical intervention). Although it doesn't offer a cure for diabetes, it can generally help many conditions that defeat orthodox medicine. Tibb takes a long-term perspective on life and tries to heal on all levels. It also aims to bring us back in balance with our environment, with the natural world. Once we follow natural rhythms and stop trying to work against the world around us, good health naturally follows. We may live in a modern world but the natural world still beats to an ancient rhythm. Tibb helps us to regain our inherent harmony.

TIBB HOME HELP

Tibb physicians believe simple changes in lifestyle can profoundly help your health and happiness. They recommend:

- Getting up early. Ideally you should rise before sunrise and certainly before 7am. Drink a little warm water and honey on rising to prevent constipation.
- Always eat a good breakfast. Skimping on or avoiding breakfast will lower your energy levels. Lunch should be a reasonable-sized meal and the evening meal should be light and eaten at least two hours before bedtime. Following this regime should also regulate your weight. Tibb teaches that most Western obesity is caused by eating too much too late at night and not enough at breakfast.
- Exercise. Like most systems of natural health, Tibb emphasises regular exercise to keep you healthy in body and mind. Walking is excellent.
- Make sure you get enough relaxation. Too many of us live in our heads and are overstimulated. If you always feel tired, try taking half an hour's siesta in the afternoon. Maybe have a warm bath with essential oils or massage your feet or head with light oils.
- Incorporate spirituality into your life. Whether it involves prayer, meditation or simple contemplation of the beauty in the world, just 10 minutes a day will help bring you peace.
- Don't go to bed too late. Our natural clock would take us to bed no more than a couple of hours after sunset. Try to be in bed by at least 11pm.
- Cultivate good sleep. If you have trouble sleeping, try meditating before sleep or experiment with gentle massage – on your feet or head. A warm milky drink is comforting. Start by sleeping on your right side to promote restful sleep.

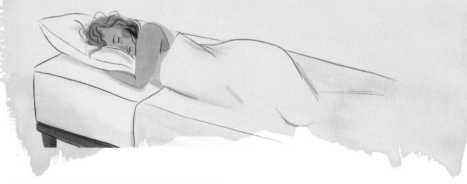

MONGOLIAN MEDICINE

Mongolian medicine goes way beyond the merely mechanical – it believes health is a fusion of physical, psychological and spiritual. It's as likely to offer prayers as pills and performs exorcisms alongside acupuncture. Could you blame your depression on a past life? Are you feeling rough because your stars are unfavourable this year? Maybe you're suffering bad luck because you're being targeted by an evil spirit?

Too crazy for modern times? Well, not necessarily. Mongolian medicine predates the concepts of quantum physics by several millennia, insisting that time is relative (the past and future affect the present) and that we are not separate from our surroundings. Evil spirits? Unhealthy projections maybe.

I was lucky enough to visit Mongolia a few years back and I will never forget the beauty of its landscape and people. Most Mongolians are nomads, living in temporary ger (a yurt-like structure) settlements. They live lightly on the earth and have a deep connection with the landscape. Many people would describe the middle of the Gobi Desert in Outer Mongolia as a desolate place, yet I have rarely felt so safe, so nurtured. This land is known, held sacred and, if you approach it with your mind and heart open, it holds you, it heals you. I lay on rocks which offered a natural form of acupressure. Quite simply, I have never felt so loved by the landscape. Mongolia's people (like all nomads) have a deep simplicity of life from which we could

learn so much. Nobody in Mongolia needs to declutter – when your entire home needs to be transported on a camel or yak cart, you can't afford to hoard. Nor do you need much in the way of material possessions when there is such incandescent joy in the patterned sky at night, in the sparks of a fire, in the plangent beauty of song.

Mongolian medicine was ancient when Genghis Khan galloped across Central Asia. At its heart is Dom, an ancient folk medicine which has been retained in its purity and offers highly unusual remedies. Horse milk is used to treat lung complaints. An infection in the umbilical cord of a newborn is cured by burning a piece of its mother's hair, grinding it into ash and putting it on the sore place – it is said to heal overnight. There are incredibly arcane formulae for everything from soothing mouth ulcers to promoting youthfulness.

Mongolian medicine is said to be as ancient, if not more so, than the great healing systems of China, Tibet, the Middle East and India. In fact, it shares

many techniques with them – the use of herbs, moxibustion (the burning of herbs on the skin), acupuncture, massage and manipulation. Even its spiritual practices are not dissimilar – although this side of traditional Eastern medicine is generally played down in the West.

Diagnosis is swift and efficient. Pulse, tongue and eye diagnosis are the main tools, as with Chinese and Ayurvedic physicians. When I visited a Mongolian physician, I found his diagnosis pretty well spot on. However, alongside dietary and herbal cures, he also offered me a healing ritual. Apparently my astrological chart showed I needed to take care of my health and finances in the coming year (I followed the advice so I'll never know what might have happened if I hadn't). Ancient parchments detailing such rituals are handed down from teacher to pupil. Ritual is considered a vital part of healing.

Massage is also used and, while very few Mongolian physicians come to the West, you may find a practitioner of chua-ka bodywork far more easily.

With its talk of spirits and exorcism, rituals and reincarnation, Mongolian medicine is easy to dismiss as quaint superstition. Yet I can't dismiss my diagnosis as superstition – or even an inspired guess – and there is no disguising the fact that my body felt simply wonderful after my chua-ka session. As Western researchers discover that much folkloric 'fiction' is actually scientific fact, maybe we should keep an open mind to Mongolian medicine – it might just help us cure our ills.

BUSH MEDICINE
THE ANCIENT WISDOM OF AUSTRALIA

A few years ago it was discovered that the most ancient continuous civilisation on earth is that of the Aboriginal and Torres Strait Islander peoples of Australia, Tasmania and the offshore islands. Just pause and think about that for a moment. There are many Aboriginal nations, each with their own language, traditions and medicine. It's a rich culture and one that stretches back as far, if not further, than those of India and China. Yet so much has been lost.

This wise culture has a totally oral tradition, passed down by word, song, dance and ritual through the generations. However an oral tradition, as rich and nuanced as it is, is desperately vulnerable. When genocide struck Australia, it destroyed millennia of knowledge alongside a truly horrific proportion of its peoples. It's estimated that, in 1788, there were around 750,000 indigenous peoples. Europeans caused the death of approximately 600,000 of them. We will never know what has been lost.

What we do know is that the first principle of what is generally called 'bush medicine' was eating well – choosing the right combinations of food, according to season, to keep in good health. The use of tonic herbs was also standard. When someone did fall ill, there was a massive pharmacy of healing plants to call upon (dependent on the region). Many of these are now being researched as their healing properties are slowly, belatedly, being understood and appreciated.

Bush medicine has always had a highly holistic view of wellbeing. Traditional healers were (and still are) part physician, part psychiatrist, part priest. Generally illness is categorised as either natural or supernatural. Natural diseases and injuries are treated with practical natural cures: plant and animal remedies; steam, clay, charcoal and mud baths; and massage. If an illness is thought to have a deeper cause, it is treated with spiritual healing and shamanic ceremonies, recognising that illness is often in the head and soul as much as in the body.

In addition, health is not considered as purely individual – it affects the wellbeing of the entire community, so healers would also settle conflicts and give out advice.

SIX KEY BUSH MEDICINES

1. **Tea tree (*Melaleuca alternifolia*):** The Bundjalung peoples of New South Wales learned that bathing in water infused with the leaves of the local tree could heal a wide variety of skin conditions. We now know that tea tree has antifungal, antiseptic and antibiotic properties.

2. **Eucalyptus (*Eucalyptus* spp.):** Several types of eucalyptus were used – mainly for treating wounds but also for relieving aches and pains in muscles, joints and even teeth. It is now recognised as possessing antiseptic, antimicrobial, antiviral, antibacterial and antifungal properties.

3. **Billy goat plum (Kakadu plum; *Terminalia ferdinandiana*):** A fruit from the woodlands of the Northern Territory and Western Australia, billy goat plum was considered a gift of the Dreamtime. It was used for its antiseptic and soothing qualities in traditional healing. An Australian superfood, it's now known to be one of the richest sources of vitamin C in the world and is rich in phytochemicals, which are only just being explored.

4. **Emu bush (*Eremophila longifolia*):** Northern Territory people used a concoction of emu bush leaves for sores and cuts, or as a gargle. Infusions were used to help colds, headaches and chest pain. It was smoked to create a sterile environment for newborn babies and their mothers. It has been found to be as strong as some antibiotics.

5. **Snake vine (*Hibbertia scandens*):** In Central and Northern Australia the leaves and stems of the vine were crushed to treat sores, wounds, headaches and inflammatory diseases such as arthritis. It was also known as 'ngalyipi'. The sap was used as an antiseptic, too.

6. **Kangaroo apple (*Solanum laciniatum*):** Part of the potato family, kangaroo apple grows in colder parts of the country and islands. It has been applied as a poultice on swollen joints for thousands of years. The plant has been found to contain a natural anti-inflammatory steroid that is important in the production of cortisone.

THE DREAMING

One essential part of Australian ancient wisdom is the Dreaming. The term itself is European as different clans of the Aboriginal and Torres Strait Islander peoples have their own names. Although it's often described as 'mythology', it is far deeper than that. The Dreaming is a world view that, once, way back, all peoples shared. It's a framework for understanding the world around us, and our place within that world.

The Dreaming provides an understanding, an explanation, of how creation came about. It also gives a set of rules for right living – ceremony, ritual, social relationships, economics even.

At the beginning of the world, the land was flat, featureless, empty. Then the ancestral spirits came up from the earth and down from the sky. They created the land in a flamboyant wild dance, each according to their nature: they crawled and scratched and swept the land; they made love, gave birth and menstruated the land. These Dreamtime creators weren't all lofty beings or mighty creatures, such as the Rainbow Serpent; they encompassed humbler ancestors – the honey ant, the termite, the spinifex hopping mouse. All are included – there is no hierarchy in creation.

The ancestor spirits gave the newly awakened people their songs and dances, their languages and rituals, their laws and codes of conduct. When their work was completed, the ancestors returned into the earth, the sky, the animals – no longer walking the land, but a part of it.

How might it feel to walk on the world as if it had life, memory, awareness? What rich connection with the land have we lost? The songlines aren't about nature, they are nature – and we humans are part of that song, not above it. In her incredible book, *Wild*, Jay Griffiths talks about how, for Aboriginal peoples, ritual and ceremony contribute to the wellbeing of the land and this, in turn, makes people happy. She says there is a word, 'punyu', in the Ngarinman language of the Yarralin people that means happy, strong, healthy, knowledgeable and socially responsible: 'It is the state of being fully alive.'

This ancient pull to revere and communicate with a sentient world still thrums through us, if we listen. It's there when we feel the urge to climb a hill and lie, our bodies sinking into the earth, our faces turned to the sky. It echoes through the folk stories, legends and myths that every country (no matter how 'sophisticated') still retains when you scratch the surface.

AFRICAN ANCIENT WISDOM

Traditional African healing is ancient, venerable, effective and still very much in use today. Obviously, given the size of the continent, there are regional variations; however, the components stay pretty much constant.

Traditional medicine is deep and broad, encompassing herbal medicine, the use of therapeutic diets and fasting, hydrotherapy, spinal manipulation, massage, psychiatry, surgery and spiritual/energy healing. Herbs are treated as the great healers they undoubtedly are. It would take an entire book to do this wisdom justice. Once again, colonisation proved disastrous both to indigenous peoples and their knowledge. As with Australia, most African wisdom is not written down in books – it's passed down orally through generations.

One aspect of African ancient wisdom that resonates powerfully in modern times is the vital importance of community. We are pack animals by nature. We need our families, our clans. Sobonfu Somé puts it so well in her book *Welcoming Spirit Home*: 'The community concept is based on the fact that each person is invaluable and truly irreplaceable. Each person has a gift to give, a contribution to make to the whole... When we are "separate" we are vulnerable and are more likely to underestimate the self.'

A few years back I attended The Bridge, a remarkable healing retreat based on modern psychotherapy combined with ancient African ritual practices. A large part of the healing comes from reconnecting participants to a 'tribe' and allowing the power of the group to work its magic. 'We are tribal beings', says Donna Lancaster, co-founder of The Bridge, 'We belong together, and healing in community is part of that.'

I have found, over my years of attending retreats, that there is a deep truth in this. Individual counselling and psychotherapy can be a hugely valuable tool but, in my experience, we go deeper and heal more swiftly and thoroughly when we work on ourselves within the safe holding of a group. When we listen, truly listen, to other people's stories, we gain insights into our own. We learn, not only empathy, but that our problems are human – shared by so many others. Working with a group, our clan, our tribe (even if it's a made-up tribe that only hangs out together for a week or so), allows us to open our hearts, to recognise the bigger picture, to be of service in the world. It's big work.

How do we do that in our manicured, cut off, isolated, individualistic lives? I think we have to find clans. Get out there and track down people you can talk to, people you can listen to. You may find that sense of belonging within a spiritual group – either of an organised religion or a more loose affiliation of spiritually inclined people. You might find a common interest – in music, singing, dancing, art, storytelling, sport, yoga, fitness. You don't have to be good at this stuff – not at all. Look for groups that play with free movement – moving the way your body wants to move, rather than making the right shapes on the dance floor. Check out art therapy where the last thing you're trying to do is to make nice neat 'art'. Look up the Red Tent movement for women's groups. Check out groups of wild women, wild men, wild people generally who get together to chew the fat around a campfire, to howl at the moon, to laugh and cry together. If you are truly isolated, you may need to find your tribe online and that's fine too. Just get connected.

ANCIENT WISDOM OF MESOAMERICA

The first complex civilisations of Central America were some of the most advanced cultures in the world. The Olmecs, thought to have come to Mesoamerica from Africa over 4,000 years ago, built extraordinary cities with pyramid structures, aqueducts and walled plazas. They had profound understanding of mathematics, engineering, farming, masonry and writing. Other famous cultures include the Aztec, the Mayan and the Inca.

All had a depth of medicinal wisdom that, like most of the ancient forms of healing, saw health as a combination of mind, body and spirit – blending physical cures with psychological and spiritual interventions. The Mayans had extensive medical knowledge – encompassing surgery and even advanced dental work. Herbal medicines were studied and were used alongside other techniques, including sweat baths (known as 'temezcal'), for healing. Once again, this is a huge subject – one I can't possibly do justice to within a few scant paragraphs.

In the last century, the Toltec spiritual tradition has come into the spotlight. The Toltecs left no written records, but modern authors such as Carlos Castaneda and Don Miguel Ruiz use the word Toltec as shorthand for the extensive ancient traditions of Mexico and Central America. The worldview is predominantly shamanic. Castaneda highlighted the use of sacred spirit 'allies' (hallucinogenic plants such as peyote and jimson weed that could help bestow knowledge and power). Ruiz combined ancient Toltec wisdom with modern psychotherapy. His best-known book is *The Four Agreements* and it contains a smart message for all of us.

THE FOUR AGREEMENTS

1. **Be impeccable.** Speak your truth, maintain your integrity and authenticity – be yourself. This is all about honesty combined with compassion. It asks that we don't gossip or bad-mouth people. That we use our words to spread truth and love.

2. **Don't make assumptions.** How much grief would we lose if we all followed this? So often we assume we know what other people think, believe, feel. Yet often we are entirely wrong. Ruiz says we should find the courage to ask people what they want, what they mean. In turn, we should communicate with other people as clearly and honestly as we can. It's so simple – yet so transformative. When in doubt (in other words, always) – ask.

3. **Don't take anything personally.** We are self-centred beings and we think the world revolves around us. Ruiz says that nothing other people do is because of us. Everything they say and do is a projection of their own reality, their own dream. Taking back responsibility for ourselves is a huge step. Imagine – instead of blaming other people ('she broke my heart'), you recognise your own choice ('I let her break my heart').

4. **Always do your best.** As Ruiz points out, our best will change from moment to moment. All you can do at any one time is your best under the circumstances.

Ruiz later added a fifth agreement – **Be sceptical, but learn to listen.**

Many people have exercised that right to be sceptical, pouring scorn on the agreements, saying they can't possibly be Toltec in origin but, frankly, I don't think it matters too much. They strike a chord with me (and with many other people) so why not use them? Learn to listen to your heart.

SOUTH AMERICAN TRADITIONS

Traditional medicine is still very much alive in wide swathes of South America. The Amazon rainforest is now under the microscope as it has belatedly been recognised as a vast herbal pharmacy. Scientists are finally accepting that traditional rainforest medicine uses plants with incredible healing properties, holding the potential to cure a wide range of diseases, from cancer to psychiatric illnesses. However thousands, if not millions, of species are being lost as the rainforest continues to be destroyed. Entire societies are being forced out of their homes, their knowledge exploited for commercial gain by the pharmaceutical companies.

These companies will seek to isolate active constituents of plants, to create drugs that can be patented and sold. They miss so much. The wise women and men of the Amazon are known as 'vegetalistas' – they don't just know about plants, they learn from plants. Plants are teachers, as in all indigenous American traditions. It's deep, it's subtle – a wisdom that can't be scrutinised on a molecular level.

Take the herbal brew, ayahuasca, which has become famous in recent years. Also known as 'natem', 'shori', 'caapi', 'yage', 'hoasca', 'vegetal', 'uni', among others, it is an ancient form of spiritual medicine used in ceremonies across the Amazon basin. The brew is traditionally made from the liana (vine) *Banisteriopsis caapi* and the chacruna shrub *Psychotria viridis*, which contains DMT (dimethyltryptamine), a psychoactive compound. However, each shaman prepares the brew in varying ways with different mixtures of plants.

Ayahuasca is considered a sacrament

and the brew works on physical, psychological and spiritual levels. It's a purgative that can induce vomiting and diarrhoea (used to help clear the body from worms and other parasites). However, it is mostly known for its psychedelic effects, which can often lead to a sense of expanded consciousness and of deep spirituality. The profound wisdom of ayahuasca is that we are not alone, we are not solitary beings – we are part of creation. When we realise our belonging in this beautiful world, we become more awake, more aware of how precious it is. Some people say they meet guides and healers, and report distinct shifts in their physical and emotional wellbeing. Early studies indicate that ayahuasca can significantly reduce the symptoms of depression.

A note of warning: ayahuasca increases heart rate and blood pressure so should be approached with caution by anyone at risk of heart disease. The popularity

of ayahuasca has also led to people
jumping on the (lucrative) bandwagon
and offering brews they are unqualified
to administer. One alternative way to
glimpse this unified vision of the universe
is a specific breathing technique known
as 'Holotropic Breathwork'®.

SHAMANISM AND RITUAL

Shamans are the sacred wisdom keepers. They are the men and women who can walk between the worlds to talk to animals, plants and both incarnate and disincarnate guides. They perform deep healing for body and soul. Every ancient culture had shamans – some still do.

The word 'shamanism' originally comes from Evenki, the language of the Tungus tribe in Siberia, but is now universally used to refer to the ancient spiritual practices of indigenous peoples all over the world. The dictionary describes it as 'a religion practiced by indigenous peoples of far northern Europe and Siberia that is characterised by a belief in an unseen world of gods, demons, and ancestral spirits responsive only to the shamans.' I don't think that definition is anywhere near inclusive enough. Shamanic traditions are found all over the world – from the Amazon rainforest to the North American plains; from the deserts of Australia to the mountains of Nepal. Shamanism is not a religion – it's a totally non-denominational method.

Japanese Shintoism has shamanic elements. I would say shamanism is firstly the fundamental belief that all of nature is connected, including us human animals. Secondly, that our health is intrinsically linked with the health of our community, both in its local sense and in the sense of our planetary family. Thirdly, that by accessing an altered state of being

we can find healing (both for ourselves, for others and for the planet). Fourthly, we are not alone – we have spirit guides and helpers who can help us with our healing work. Maybe the hardest concept to grasp is that, by doing work in the spirit realms, we can affect change in this material world.

In many traditions, the shaman was the medicine man or woman, the magician, the sorcerer, the wizard or witch, the seer. In many Western cultures, they were feared and hunted (witness the horrific witch trials – the murder of the wise women and men across Europe). Now we are witnessing a resurgence of interest in this ancient shared wisdom. It's wonderful to see.

We aren't all drawn to the shamanic path in this life (it is a tough and arduous training), but we can use its teachings to deepen our link with the world around us and to Spirit. I have undertaken several shamanic trainings (which still makes me a total novice) and find the work powerful, profound and curiously comforting – it links me in with the wider world.

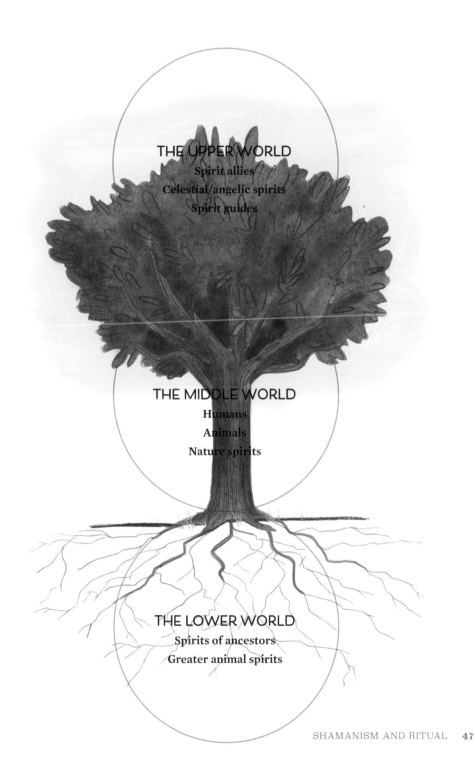

THE UPPER WORLD
Spirit allies
Celestial/angelic spirits
Spirit guides

THE MIDDLE WORLD
Humans
Animals
Nature spirits

THE LOWER WORLD
Spirits of ancestors
Greater animal spirits

THE THREE REALMS

Traditionally there are three main spirit realms:

The Lower World: sometimes known as the Place of Death but it's not usually a dark frightening place. This is where you commonly meet animal guides, spirit animals. It's also the realm where you can meet the souls of your ancestors. In addition, it's the place which may hold parts of your soul that have become lost or cut off through trauma. Soul retrieval has always been a part of shamanistic practice – now it's being recognised as vital in the healing of trauma.

The Middle World: this is a parallel world to our material world – here you find information and answers about this world and life. In this world you can see people, animals and places that exist now. You can ask for information to help you understand people and situations better.

The Upper World: this is a world of clouds and light, filled with what could be termed angels, spirits, wise beings. Here you can ask for guidance from higher beings with an overview of life. You would tend to ask for spiritual wisdom and advice here, rather than focusing on more mundane matters.

To access these worlds, you need to take yourself into a trance state. This is done by relaxing your body, shutting out the light and following the insistent beat of a drum or rattle. Visualisation takes you to the world you want to access, where you will meet guides. I will guide you through a typical journey later in the book (pages 157–159).

It's worth pointing out that you don't have to become a fully-fledged shaman to benefit from a shamanic world view. Throughout the book, I will also offer some 'entry level' shamanic rituals and practices that give a taste of the work. If you're interested in taking it further, I'd thoroughly recommend *The Way of the Shaman*, by Michael Harner, a pioneer of shamanism in the West. There are also many shamanic schools offering workshops and trainings – but do exercise some caution when choosing your path. Any leader with a large following may fall into the shadow side (you can see it even with yoga teachers and some 'gurus'). Use your common sense, check in with your heart and gut at all times.

An important part of the shamanic life is the role of ritual and ceremony. Modern research shows that collective rituals create major neural changes, synchronising the hemispheres of the brain. Being part of a meaningful ceremony helps us become more emotionally resilient. It has also been shown to deepen our connection to other people and to the world around us. Now, more than ever, we need this renewed sense of connection, meaning and purpose. So I'll be introducing some simple forms of ritual and ceremony throughout the book for you to try.

NATUROPATHY

Naturopathy is to the West what Ayurveda and Traditional Chinese Medicine are to the East – a gentle, nature-based, holistic health system that aims to put the whole body in balance. Many of its 'cures' involve simple DIY routines that can be incorporated into every regime.

Historically speaking, the roots of naturopathy lie in darkest antiquity. Hippocrates spoke of 'ponos', the body's incessant labour to restore itself to normal balance, while Aristotle spoke of the life force having a purpose beyond simply existing.

Naturopathy is the great cleansing therapy. It blames many of our problems on incomplete elimination of the waste products of our metabolism and the accumulation of toxins. The body tries to live with it and the result is low-level 'dis-ease' – not a particular illness but a sense of feeling below par. So the aim of all naturopathic processes is to help the elimination of waste, bolstering every one of the body's excretory functions. It has a vast storehouse of diets, detox treatments, water therapies and exercise regimes.

Balance is achieved by using the most natural cures available: fresh air and sunlight, fasting and a fresh clean diet, relaxation and psychological counselling and, very importantly, the healing power of water. In addition, many naturopaths are also trained osteopaths and will deal with mechanical problems with a course of manipulation.

Nowadays many naturopaths add to this basic repertoire by including medical herbalism and homeopathy.

If you want to experience a full naturopathic cure, you should head to mainland Europe, where systems such as the Mayr cure have taken naturopathic principles and turned them into a system of healing. The 'cure' is pretty stringent, but you come out feeling light and bright in both body and mind.

HOW TO USE THIS BOOK

**I've organised the material around the seasons for the reasons I've already cited.
I think it's vital we recognise that we are creatures like any others –
our bodies and minds are still ruled by nature, we hum to the
deep beat of the year's cycle.**

Coming back into tune with these natural rhythms, even in the smallest ways, can have a huge knock-on effect on our health and happiness. I also love this format as it offers a pleasing, easily followed structure to our year. However, as you'll see, there is a lot of crossover and so feel free to dip in and out, to plunge forwards and refer backwards as you feel the urge. Listen for the age-old wisdom of your heart and gut. Once you feel that, you won't go far wrong.

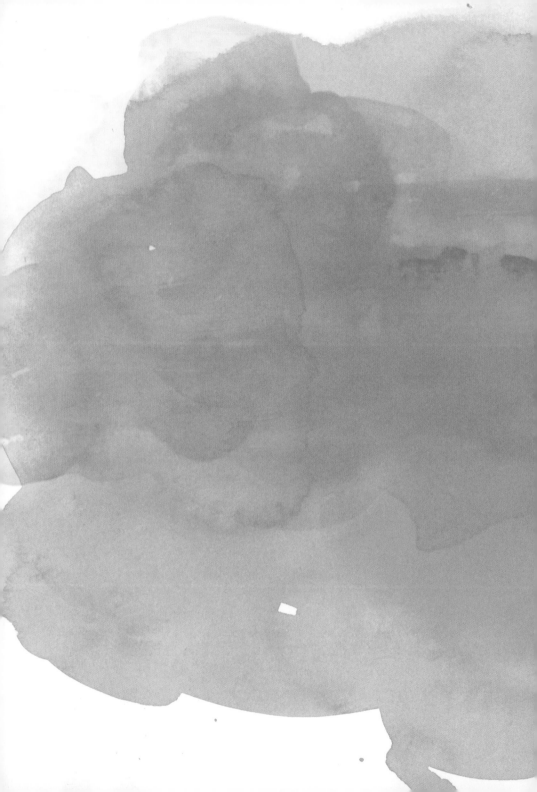

SPRING

INTRODUCTION

Who doesn't love spring? It arrives with a lilting song of 'wake up', gently urging us to shrug off the inward quiet of winter and stretch our arms to the bright new energy. It's the season of fresh life, new beginnings, hope and vigour. Everything is growing in spring – the sap is rising, roots are expanding, vital energy (qi, prana) is rising too. No wonder we feel the urge for spring cleaning – this is the natural time to cleanse our bodies, our minds, our emotions and our space.

In the ancient Chinese system, spring is considered the season of the element wood. It is full to the brim with the explosive energy of 'young yang'. Think of this energy as a young person, desperate to break free of the family nest and to spring out into the world, full of wild energy and the desire to change the world yet not quite sure of their limits and boundaries. It's a wonderful, exciting energy but can be just a tad reckless.

Wood challenges us to be our own people, to follow our dreams and stick fast to our integrity. It lures us into meeting new people; to try new things; to dare, to stretch, to explore, to tiptoe (or race) outside our comfort zone.

However, it can start to dominate, leading to feelings of obsession, of being out of control. Not for nothing do we have the term 'spring fever'.

The colour associated with wood is green and its direction, unsurprisingly, is the east – the direction of the dawn, the start of each fresh day. In Chinese wisdom, the secondary element associated with spring is wind. Think of wind as the brisk gusty breezes of spring – blowing away all that is old and unnecessary and ushering in the new. Often we will unconsciously throw open our windows to welcome in this bright new, no-nonsense energy. However, be cautious. The 'evil' of spring is unbalanced wind. If we've taken care of ourselves over the cold winter months, it should pose no problems. Yet if we're run down, our energy low and stagnant, wind and wood can throw our balance out even more. Watch out for spring colds, coughs and even bouts of flu. Balancing yourself through each season will prevent this happening next year.

Eastern healers learned, thousands of years ago, that two organs are stimulated each season, in order to become cleansed and re-energised. In spring, these are the liver, which has many roles including filtering the blood, and the gall bladder, which stores and concentrates bile. The liver is connected to our eyes, blood and tendons. When this is out of balance we can feel irritable and even angry, unable to digest our feelings. This can sometimes affect our drive in life and manifest as the 'blues'. When the gall bladder meridian is out of balance we can lack courage, we just can't seem to judge things very well. We might wake in the night and not be able to get back to sleep. We might have a stiff neck and ringing in the ears. We feel timid and indecisive.

In this section, we'll look at how to balance these meridians. We'll investigate how to ease your diet into spring, to make the most of the fresh new season's produce. We'll take it a bit deeper too, seeing how herbal tonics can boost your immune system and prepare your body for the new season's energy.

Spring is all about expansion, so we'll be focusing on deep stretching with yoga and introducing a simple flow sequence that is tailor-made to ease you into spring. Our bodywork continues the strong, lean, stretching theme with a look at acupressure, shiatsu and one of my all-time favourite massage therapies, the South Indian art of 'chavutti thirumal'.

Spring is the traditional time in ancient cultures across the world to clean and cleanse. We retain an element of that with spring cleaning, however ancient wisdom goes much deeper. We'll look at how to give your home an energetic makeover with space clearing and smudging. You'll notice a palpable difference. We'll take a walk on the wild side with the shamanic art of medicine walking. Then we end with a look at (or rather a sound of) sound healing. From gong baths to toning mantras, from singing bowls to deep groaning – you'll find the sounds that make your soul expand.

SPRING DIET

In Ayurveda, it's said that how you eat in spring will dictate your health for the whole of the year. We tend to go into spring with an excess of stolid, heavy kapha energy – thanks to our heavier diet over the cold winter months, often combined with less exercise. Now it's time to lighten up. Your key words for spring cooking are light, dry, fresh, warm. No more carb-laden comfort food. Keep everything warm though – salads are fine but incorporate something cooked to keep some heat (warm rice, pan-roasted vegetables, stir-fried tofu, etc.). Think soups rather than smoothies.

The tastes to emphasise now are bitter and pungent. Dark green leafy vegetables are absolutely perfect – they're so good, in fact, that many cultures use them as tonics. Use every opportunity you can to bring them into your diet – lightly steam them and add to Buddha bowls or stir-fries; use them to boost soups and make light delicate spring stews (barley and rice add some grounding stability

but aren't too heavy).

If you're a meat-eater, stick to chicken, turkey and rabbit at this time of year (red meat is just too heavy). A little fish is fine too. When choosing grains, look to those that are light and dry in nature – amaranth, barley, buckwheat, quinoa and basmati rice are ideal. It's the same story with legumes – go for aduki, black, navy, pinto and white beans. Chickpeas, black-eyed peas, split peas and red lentils are great too. Tofu should be cooked at this time of year – the energy of cold soy products is too damp for spring. Equally, this isn't the time of year to go heavy on nuts but you can add seeds, in particular chia, flax, pumpkin and sunflower seeds.

Go very easy on dairy produce – it's heavy in nature and can be mucus-forming for many people. If you can't live without your yogurt, try goat or sheep yogurt (they're much lighter) or tangy kefir. Coconut 'yogurt' is another option.

Spice up spring every way you can. In particular, focus on ginger, garlic, chilli, coriander (ideally the fresh leaves) and cayenne pepper. Mustard greens, radish and sprouts are also good for adding crunch and pack a dry, warming punch. Ginger tea is ideal for warming the body in spring. It also boosts 'agni', our digestive fire. A cup of hot water with a teaspoon of honey can help balance any stodgy kapha energy.

Take care with your cooking and avoid using too much oil. Even ghee, so beloved of Ayurvedic cooking, is kept to a minimum during spring.

SPRING CLEANSE

Spring is the perfect time to give our bodies a gentle cleanse. This isn't a draconian detox – it's simply a chance to let your body release what it doesn't need for the brighter, lighter days ahead. I was first introduced to this kind of cleanse when I met Fiona Arrigo, a psychotherapist and master healer who launched one of the first modern transformative retreats, all based on ancient wisdom. Fiona is now renowned globally for her work.

In a nutshell, the golden rules are: eat seasonally, eat naturally, eat mindfully and keep hydrated, which means eating organic veg and fruit and seeds, lean protein, legumes, whole grains, herbs and spices and herbal teas. Try to avoid the deadly nightshade family (potatoes, aubergine, peppers and tomatoes), oranges, rhubarb and grapefruit, red meat, dairy, shellfish, alcohol and caffeine, wheat, sugary and processed foods. Follow this regime for at least a week for good results. If you feel well, with good energy, feel free to continue for longer.

TONICS

Spring time is tonic time. Because the energy of the season is so strong, it's common in China to balance the body with a herb or combination of herbs. If you can see a practitioner for a tailor-made tonic, so much the better (though be warned, some Chinese herb mixtures are pretty disgusting). However, you can go a long way on your own simply by adding healing herbs to your soups and salads.

Tonic herbs are known as adaptogens. They bring the body into balance. A 'normal' herb will always do the same thing – for example, it might lower blood pressure regardless of whether your blood pressure is low or high. However, a tonic herb will aim to balance each individual body, normalising or regulating organs and systems. They also help to 'stress-proof' the body by strengthening the immune system, and increase energy by supporting the metabolism, rather than artificially stimulating it.

Many tonic herbs have their own specialist subject – for the blood, for the digestive system and so on. A good tonic usually comprises several different herbs, tailored to your specific needs. It's like a bespoke spring clean for the body.

The idea of taking herbs when you're not specifically sick can be hard to grasp – this idea of preventative medicine is a concept that, sadly, Western medicine doesn't tend to adopt.

CHINESE HERBAL TONICS

Treat these healers with care and caution – herbs are powerful medicine and should be treated with respect. If you have any concerns, any medical condition or are pregnant or breastfeeding, it's essential you see a well-qualified practitioner. If you're on medication, check with your physician.

Astragalus (huang qi; *Astragalus membranaceus*)

Astragalus has been used for thousands of years to tone and strengthen the body. It is primarily known as a heart tonic, used to balance blood pressure, strengthen the heart by increasing the flow of blood to it and to help prevent diabetes. It is also renowned as an immune-enhancer and is a traditional remedy for depression.

Ginseng

There are several types of ginseng, but both the Asian and American (*Panax quinquefolius*) contain the same active compounds, known as ginsenosides. Ginseng is known as a 'cure all', a powerful tonic for the whole body. It was specifically used to improve the immune system, protect the heart and boost energy and concentration. Note: Siberian ginseng (*Eleutherococcus senticosus*) contains different active compounds, known as eleutherosides.

Chinese angelica (dang gui; *Radix Angelicae sinensis*)

Commonly known as 'female ginseng', dang gui is traditionally used for menopausal and menstrual problems; it is said to nourish the blood and encourage circulation. It may also help alleviate tiredness, fever, headaches and irritability.

Goji (gou qi zi; *Fructus lycii*)

Also known as 'wolfberry', the small red berries are commonly used in Chinese medicine for liver and kidney weakness, for weak vision and for sexual dysfunction. They are also used to relieve chronic coughs. Above all, goji is renowned for its gentle energising properties. It is often advised after illness as it strengthens the body. Goji is also renowned as a tonic for menopausal women, treating fatigue and vaginal dryness.

Schisandra (Wu wei zi; *Fructus Schisandrae chinensis*)

Schisandra is a famous liver, kidney and sexual tonic for both men and women, with the added benefit of softening the skin. It is also said to increase endurance and reduce fatigue.

TONICS FROM THE GARDEN

Many tonic herbs are often overlooked as weeds. They were used by early herbalists to help the body recover from a long season of dried and salted foods. They support elimination and are fantastic skin and liver tonics, so give them a try (with, of course, caution). UK foraging expert Adele Nozedar recommends these:

Nettle (*Urtica dioica*)

Nettles are rich in protein and vitamin C. Use them as you would spinach – in soups, omelettes, stir-fries or make a syrup. Although they will act as a general tonic for everyone, clinical trials have shown nettles can help heart problems, and are useful for prostrate problems, asthma, hay fever and hives.

Dandelion (*Taraxacum officinalis*)

Dandelion is a natural diuretic that helps flush out toxins. It's a blood, liver and kidney cleanser. Use the leaves in salads or soups; or make dandelion tea – just put a handful of washed leaves in a teapot, add boiling water and steep for 5 minutes. It's bitter so you might want to add some mint leaves to balance.

Cleavers (*Galium aparine*)

Also known as goosegrass, these are long, whip-like plants with very sticky stalks. They are soothing to the gut and a powerful anti-inflammatory. Use the young leaves (not the stalks) either raw in salads, steamed or sautéed.

YOGA
THE BIG STRETCH

Spring is the season for deep stretching. It's time to wake up and move. In ancient cultures, of course, there would be no need to say that – our ancestors moved (a lot) as part of their everyday lives. Nobody needed a gym in ancient India, Tibet or on the North American plains. In our sedentary Western world, however, we have lost the art of natural movement.

In addition to everyday activity, the ancients discovered that moving in particular ways brought additional benefits. Yoga stretches back at least 5,000 years (some researchers think it may be twice as old), and was first mentioned in the Vedas, the sacred Indian texts.

What we think of as yoga (the physical postures known as 'asanas') are only one limb of the yogic tree. Its original purpose was to ease our bodies and minds into an awareness of their own nature. It was often used as a precursor to meditation as it can be tough to sit calmly unless the body has been fully stretched. However, other benefits were soon noticed. The asanas systematically put pressure on all the organs of the body, toning and nourishing. They stretch out all the muscles and ligaments, re-aligning and re-energising. Yoga boosts the circulation of both blood and our slow-moving lymph, and acts as a natural detoxifier of mind and body. It also has a powerful influence on the mind, and studies have shown yoga can help ease depression, stress and anxiety.

Nowadays, sadly, yoga isn't always the clean clear path of old. It has gained a reputation for being egotistical (even narcissistic). Some teachers are fêted as gurus and some classes can feel very intimidating if you aren't suitably gymnastic and if you don't have the latest yoga gear.

Don't let that put you off. Please. You may need to hunt around a little to find a teacher and class that suits but, once you do, you'll never look back. There is a yoga style for everyone and a good teacher will make you welcome and comfortable, however unbendy you may be.

By the way, if you really don't like yoga, don't panic. I'll introduce other forms of movement throughout the book.

WHICH YOGA?

It's entirely up to you. I'd suggest you browse around YouTube and watch videos of the different styles first. I'd always advise beginners to go to a class, rather than going it alone. It is perfectly possible to injure yourself in yoga and a good teacher will make sure your alignment is good, and that you aren't running the risk of harm. You need to find your 'edge' – the point where you feel comfortably stretched but not in any kind of pain. Pain is a clear warning signal from your body, shouting, 'Don't go there!' Remember, all bodies are different and just because the rest of your class is squatting right down to the ground, that doesn't mean you can or should.

Here are a few of the many styles on offer:

Hatha: the basic form of physical yoga and always a good entry point for beginners. Classes will usually include a variety of asanas – some in the form of flows (where you move in a series of poses without pause) and some held poses. With any luck you'll also get a bit of meditation and some deep relaxation.

Ashtanga: famed for its swift-paced, tough and highly structured sessions, it suits those who want a physically intense workout. I often find that young people and 'alpha' types who might find slower forms of yoga 'boring' will enjoy ashtanga and find it a good entry point.

Iyengar: highly precise, slow and focused, Iyengar uses a lot of props (belts, blocks, incline boards) to get you into exact alignment. Good for those who are put off by the spiritual elements of yoga.

Yin: a very slow meditative class in which you hold postures for 5 minutes or more. Highly therapeutic for the body and also used to help with psychological issues.

Jivamukti: a relatively new brand of yoga that fuses a strong gymnastic yoga practice with chanting and spiritual teachings. Fun if you want to challenge yourself and you're strong and fit.

Bikram (hot): a standardised series of two breathing exercises and 24 poses in a room heated to around 36–42°C. It's sweaty and athletic, but not remotely contemplative.

Kundalini: this one is a bit Marmite. Every class has a different focus and you will move through a series of dynamic flows, often accompanied by chanting. It's great if you're not a bendy person and can be ideal for shy beginners as it's mostly carried out with eyes shut.

SPRING YOGA

The meridians connected with spring are those of the liver and gall bladder. So our spring yoga sequence works on rebalancing their energy by releasing tension in the neck, opening the sides of the body and lengthening the insides of the legs. Each of the seasonal yoga sessions in this book has been especially designed by yoga teacher Dainei Tracy to fit with the season and its challenges.

Practise them with as much attention and awareness as you can. Don't race through.

This is also a good time of year to become acquainted with the area of the lower belly known as the 'hara'. You can help to ground the wild spring energy by bringing your awareness into this powerful generator of vital energy.

1. Sit comfortably on a firm high cushion. Either sit cross-legged or kneeling (in the posture known in the Zen tradition as 'seiza'). Use as much support as you require. You can put cushions or bolsters under your knees – you really do need to be comfortable – you are supposed to be releasing tension after all.

2. Focus on the area below your navel. Bring your breath to that part of the body. As you breathe out, consciously relax and lengthen the exhale. Practise for several minutes until you feel calm and relaxed.

3. Allow your right ear to move gently towards your right shoulder as you reach your left arm behind your back and catch hold of the inner right arm just above the elbow. Gently draw the right arm back.

This opens the upper chest at the same time as it increases the space between ear and shoulder. Repeat on the other side. You can repeat this 3 or 4 times.

4. Come back to the centre, keeping your neck long and your shoulders soft and relaxed. Now allow your jaw to drop open. Very slowly and gently tilt your head up and back. Go just as far as it takes to gain a comfortable stretch, then close the mouth, bringing your teeth together. You will feel this all round the neck and into the jaw.

5. Now let's focus on the eyes and ears. Rub your palms briskly together until you've generated plenty of heat and then place them over your eye sockets. Do this several times until your eyes feel nourished. Now do the same thing for your ears. Follow up by giving yourself an ear massage. Hold the entire ear, gently kneading and pulling. If you find places that are sore, give them more attention – until the soreness melts away.

6. Now we move onto balancing the gall bladder meridian with a posture called Easy Twist. Put your cushion and props

aside and lie on your right side. Your legs are together with knees bent. Fold them up towards your upper body as far as is comfortable, letting them rest on the floor. Now allow your left shoulder to open backwards into a gentle twist. If it's comfortable you can stretch your left arm out along the floor (either straightening it or keeping it bent, depending on what feels good for you). If it doesn't meet the mat, lay it gently across the side of your head. Your right arm can be placed wherever feels comfortable, depending on how your body moves into this twist. Hold the twist, breathing deeply and evenly for 5 or 6 breaths. Repeat on the other side. Notice any difference between the two sides.

7. Now we turn our attention to the liver meridian. A variation on the Straight Angle pose (Samakonasana) can help rebalance this meridian. Sit upright on your mat with your legs straight in front of you. You may want to pull back the bottom of your buttocks so you're sitting taller. Now widen the space between your legs, lengthening through to the toes. Experiment with how wide you can go, but don't move into any strain. Lift up your left arm so it brushes your left ear and now slowly bend towards the toes on your right foot. Really focus on lifting up before you fold over, rather than collapsing into this pose. It doesn't matter one jot how far you get. As you open up the left hand side of your body, take your breath into the hara and all along that extended side. Release slowly and gently on the out breath. Now repeat on the other side.

8. Gently bring yourself to standing. Start by taking your feet as wide apart as feels comfortable and then slowly fold forwards into a Wide Legged Forward Bend (Prasarita Padottanasana).

9. Next we move into Side Lunge pose (Skandasana). You can place your hands on the floor or use one or several blocks for support. Bend your right leg into a half squat. The knee moves directly out over the foot to avoid strain on the knee and ankle. Flex the foot of the left straight leg so that you are balancing on that heel with your toes pointing upwards. Feel your way into it as far as is comfortable for you and your body, using your hands to balance. If you feel confident and balanced, bring the upper body upright. Take your arms behind you and grasp the opposite elbows with your hands. This opens out the front of the body further, benefitting the liver meridian.

10. Straighten your right leg as you shift the weight onto the left leg and repeat the pose on the other side. Take your time and always listen to your body. As our sap rises and we quicken, it is all too easy to overdo things.

11. Sit quietly to end. After you've stretched your body is a great time to sit in meditation or just quiet contemplation. Listen to your mind and see what comes up, demanding attention. Sometimes what arises into our awareness is our own inner guru – it is always good to have confidence in this wisdom and to develop it.

BODYWORK

Most of us enjoy a pamperfest at the spa but maybe we don't always think about exactly why it feels so good. As humans, we need touch. Plenty of studies have shown clearly that babies who are starved of touch, who are not held and stroked and cuddled, fail to thrive. While lack of touch doesn't have quite such a severe effect on us adults, even the simplest massage can have quantifiable results. Levels of stress hormones drop right down, levels of 'feel-good' hormones rise.

Ancient wisdom knew all this and more. All the great healing traditions of the world include some form of healing touch. They go far beyond simple soothing – bringing about subtle yet powerful shifts in the body and, hence, also in the mind and emotions. Maybe we shouldn't call them bodywork so much as 'soulwork'.

As with yoga, it's not a case of 'one size fits all' and you may once more need to shop around to find your perfect body healer. There has to be a deep level of trust before your body will allow itself to be held and stroked and manipulated (in the nicest possible way). So choose with care. Generally speaking, most people can benefit from bodywork. However, if you have any health conditions or issues, and certainly if you are pregnant, you will need to check with your practitioner before booking.

THAI HEALING MASSAGE

This really is the most delicious full body stretch you'll get. It's been dubbed 'lazy yoga' or 'passive yoga' because it reaps all the benefits of a solid yoga session without you needing to do a thing.

The therapist pulls and flexes, stretching and soothing you into positions you'd never imagine trying on your own.

Thai massage was said to be created around 2,500 years ago by Shivago Komarpaj, a legendary northern Indian physician said to be a friend of the Buddha. I love to imagine the Buddha having this done to him.

This method doesn't just release tension in the soft tissue of the body, it balances the energy lines of the body, known in the Thai tradition as 'sen' lines (they correspond with the Chinese meridians). Imagine the therapist's hands, feet, elbows (yes, they use all three) working to target acupressure points. The aim is to allow your qi, life force, to run smoothly around the body. The deep stretching improves flexibility and also helps the circulation of both blood and lymph.

You'll be lying on a mat on the floor rather than on a massage couch. If you're uneasy about baring all, this is the massage for you – you don't need to strip off but rather wear loose comfortable clothing. This can be a strong massage so ask your therapist to go gently if you're new to bodywork.

SHIATSU/ACUPRESSURE

Where did the use of pressure points originate? Nobody really knows and certainly India, China and Egypt would all claim that they were the first to realise that pressing on certain parts of the body could bring about amazing healing effects.

There's a rather wonderful legend that beings known as the 'Sons of Reflected Light' came to China around 10,000 BCE. These beings were said to be around seven feet tall and they founded schools of incredible healing. It was believed that they could see both the aura and the meridians of people, with the acupoints showing up as tiny points of light. So these ancient healers could see what was wrong with the body and its energy field, and could then heal by directing their own life force at the sick person, from several feet away.

Over the centuries, the story goes, this incredible sensitivity and power was diluted. Healers needed to work closer to the body and started to use pressure on the various points. This eventually was finessed to become acupuncture. Acupuncture became the medicine of the nobility while acupressure was the province of so-called 'barefoot practitioners', intuitive healers who travelled from village to village.

Shiatsu came to Japan around the sixth century CE, with the arrival of Buddhism. Delegations went from Japan to China to bring back learning and, in particular, the Chinese skills in medicine. Inevitably, over the years, the two practices grew apart, while maintaining similarities.

Nowadays, you are most likely to find shiatsu as a stand-alone therapy. If you're new to bodywork, it's a great place to start as you don't need to strip off and the practitioner will work within your pain threshold. Yet it's not a soft option by any means – expect to be pressed, moved and held in various positions. As with Thai massage, you may also find your therapist uses her or his elbows, feet and knees to gain traction.

CHAVUTTI THIRUMAL

The massage originated in southern India and was developed to keep practitioners of martial arts and dance supple and flexible. Dancers and fighters would receive a ten-day intensive course of chavutti before performances, so they could perform in peak condition and help prevent injuries and strains.

It is probably one of the most satisfying massages because it reaches pretty much every part of the body. It certainly stretches out all the muscles and ligaments of the body while stimulating the circulation of both blood and lymph.

Chavutti is not for shrinking violets. You strip off completely (some practitioners will give you a loin cloth, others leave you naked) and lie on a mat on the floor. Your body is liberally doused with oil (sesame is the standard choice). The practitioner uses a rope slung across the room for balance (this massage is sometimes referred to as the 'Indian rope massage') and uses her or his feet to sweep down the whole of one side of your body – from the tip of your outstretched fingers, up over the shoulders and down the back, hips, thighs to the toes.

Clever feet can do all that hands can do and more. Once you've experienced the solid pressure and control of a trained pair of feet, few standard massages will match. Yes, some parts might feel a little achy, but overall you feel as if you've truly been ironed out. I also found that it made me feel happier about my body image, more confident somehow. So it's no surprise to hear that chavutti is well-known for helping to build self-esteem.

AROMATHERAPY

Essential oils were used across a wide swathe of ancient cultures. The Egyptians used aromatic oils in mummification and pots of scented unguents were found in Tutankhamun's tomb. In Tell el-Amarna, aromatic herbs were burned in public places to purify the air, while people anointed themselves with animal fat mixed with aromatic oils.

The Greeks took over the practice of this early aromatherapy and Hippocrates wrote in the fourth century BCE that, 'The way to good health is to have an aromatic bath and scented massage every day'. It's a great prescription. He taught that certain aromatic oils were protection against contagious diseases – well ahead of his time, as we now know that many essential oils have antibacterial and antiviral properties.

The knowledge then passed to Arabia. Abu Bakr Muhammad Ibn Zakariya al-Razi (865–925 CE) included many herbal and aromatic formulae in his books, and Abu Ali al-Husayn Ibn Sina (mainly known today as Avicenna) used chamomile, lavender and camphor, amongst others, and is credited with discovering the method of distilling essential oils.

If you can, seek out a fully trained aromatherapist. She or he will take a full case history and can tailor your treatment according to your precise needs. Massage is the commonest form of treatment – the oils, diluted with a carrier oil, are absorbed by the skin and then circulate all around the body.

Essential oils are serious medicine. Many have potent effects on the body and, particularly if you have any health issues, you should be very careful. Some are contraindicated if you have, for example, high or low blood pressure, if you suffer from heart problems or epilepsy, or if you're pregnant or breastfeeding.

Warnings aside, I'd certainly encourage you to build up your own collection of healing oils and start using them around the home.

YOUR AROMATHERAPY STARTER KIT

Lavender: If you only buy one oil, make it lavender. It smells delicious and has a host of healing properties. Lavender is antiseptic and can swiftly soothe a burn. Healing and purifying, balancing and soothing, it gives resolution in difficult times and helps to release negative emotions. It can ease stress, soothe depression and aid peaceful sleep. A few drops of lavender in your bedtime bath will help you relax. A few drops on your pillow will send you sweet dreams.

Geranium: This is the feel-good oil – it balances the emotions, can help lift a low mood and makes you feel uplifted yet relaxed. This lovely oil stimulates the lymphatic system and can help the body eliminate fluids. It also has a hormone-balancing effect and can be very useful if you suffer from PMS. Folklore claims geranium can keep away evil spirits. Geranium works well blended with lavender when you want a calm yet happy atmosphere (for family gatherings or children's parties perhaps).

Sandalwood: It has been considered sacred for thousands of years. In the East it was used as an aid to meditation, to ease anxiety and insomnia, and even to speed the souls of the dead to heaven. It is very soothing and can be used in bath-time and bedtime blessings. Use it to ease coughs and sore throats.

Grapefruit, lemon, lime, orange, mandarin: The citrus oils are all wonderful for lifting the spirits. They also tend to be cheaper than many oils, so you can use them liberally. These are bright, cheery, stimulating oils that work well as party oils and for enlivening the home. Also think of them when you want to deal with stress but need to keep alert: they are great balancers. They are a powerful bactericide. Be cautious when using in baths – some people find they irritate the skin.

Tea tree: Tea tree is a powerful antifungal, antiviral and antibacterial. A few drops in the bath (also add some black pepper oil if you have it) can often stop a cold in its tracks. Give yourself a steam when you feel congested – it's great for clearing catarrh and may also ease sinusitis. Dilute it and use as a wash for acne. Dab on athlete's foot (it's one oil you can use neat on the skin with caution).

Ylang-ylang: It is a renowned aphrodisiac, yet it's also a supremely soothing and calming oil. Spritz it around your home when you have a party and watch the mood go seriously mellow. Ylang-ylang also promotes confidence so can be useful if you have an exam or a problem to face – put it on your diffuser or add to a tissue and tuck it into your sleeve or under your bra strap.

Peppermint: If you've got a stomach ache or are feeling a bit sick, massage your tummy with a well-diluted (1–2 drops in a dessertspoon of carrier oil) peppermint oil. It's also a great first-aid remedy for shock – pop a few drops on a tissue and inhale. Peppermint really does 'pep' you up, so it's lovely added to a shower mitt first thing in the morning, but be wary of including it in night-time baths – it's too stimulating.

HOW TO USE ESSENTIAL OILS

Aromatherapy is incredibly versatile. Your imagination is the only limit, but here are a few of my favourites:

Bathe: Make up your own bath oils and save a small fortune. You need to dilute them in either a carrier oil (I tend to use sweet almond) or milk – use a couple of tablespoons. Six drops of essential oil per bath is plenty – you'll be surprised at how powerful the scent is. This is where you can get creative, choosing either one or a mix of your favourite oils, or picking oils for a specific reason. Play safe and do a patch test before you jump in the tub.

Massage: Experiment with your favourite blends or make a specific blend for common issues. Dilute in the same ratio as the bath oil and, again, do a patch test.

Diffuse: Essential oils have been used as room cleansers and mood lifters since Egyptian times and they are way nicer than any synthetic home fragrance. You're inundated with choice these days for diffusers and vaporisers.

Clean: Years ago, when I was researching my book *Spirit of the Home*, I discovered the wonders of essential oils for cleaning. Add essential oils to your vacuum cleaner (geranium oil always cheers me up) and to your washing up liquid (I tend to use about 10 drops per bottle – with a mix of lime, orange, bergamot and grapefruit). Add a few drops of cedarwood, sandalwood, pine or rosewood to furniture polish.

Spritz: You know those little misters you get for spritzing your house plants? Add a few drops of your favourite oils to the water and you've got your own room mist. Just don't use it on the plants!

Launder: Add 3–4 drops of essential oil to the softener compartment of your washing machine. Lavender, Roman chamomile or neroli are fabulous for bed linen. If you fancy something a bit more sensual, try ylang-ylang. If there are bugs doing the rounds, opt for eucalyptus or pine. Tumble-dry your clothes with scent by adding 2 drops of oil onto a handkerchief or other small bit of fabric (it will stain so don't choose anything precious) and adding to the load.

Inhale: If you're bunged up and congested, give yourself a steam. Simply fill a bowl with just boiled water and add a few drops of eucalyptus and tea tree oils. Pop a big towel over your head and the bowl, keeping your eyes shut. Breathe deeply for as long as you feel comfortable.

SPACE CLEARING

Every form of ancient wisdom recognises subtle energy. As we've already discussed, in China it's called qi. In Japan it is known as 'ki', in India as 'prana', in the Middle East as 'qawa'. These ancient cultures have always recognised that absolutely everything around us – whether a rock, a rabbit, a table, our own body – is made of energy, vibrating at different frequencies.

Spring is a wonderful time to look at how this energy moves in our homes. While the old idea of a 'spring clean' lives on, nowadays we tend to limit our cleansing to the physical realm. In ancient cultures, cleansing the space itself, shifting its energy, was equally important – if not more so.

Most traditional cultures have a history of using space clearing techniques. From Africa to North America, from New Zealand to India, from Bali to Tibet, people have used sound, scent, prayer and intent to cleanse and balance the energy of their spaces. Even in our so-called 'modern' culture, we retain vestiges of old wisdom: the incense that is wafted around a church cleanses the atmosphere; the bottle of champagne that crashes into a new ship is a consecration ritual; the bells that ring out for Sunday prayer were originally intended to

cleanse the parish through sound.

I have been cleansing space (and myself) for nigh on 30 years now. I have been lucky enough to meet and undertake training with two great space clearers: Karen Kingston, who draws on the ancient wisdom of the Balinese culture, and Denise Linn, who worked for years learning techniques from the Hawaiian Hunas and from teachers in the Native American tradition.

Just imagine if you hadn't physically cleaned your house for, say, five years: it would be absolutely filthy. Now just think that most houses in the West have not been energetically cleared in hundreds of years – if at all. It's an uncomfortable thought. Space clearers believe that many of the problems we have in life – bad health, difficult relationships, low energy – can be caused by living in places with stuck energy.

We can all practise simple space healing techniques.

CLEANING

Clean right through your home from top to bottom, clearing any clutter as you go. Use natural cleaning products – you really don't want to put unpleasant chemicals into your environment. As I said earlier, I love to use essential oils as I clean.

CLAPPING

Now your home is clean and fresh, it's time to start the more esoteric work. Always keep a window open when you work for any negative energy to move out of your space. Take off jewellery and keep your feet bare. It's not advisable to undertake space clearing if you are menstruating, pregnant or feeling below par. Energy can easily become 'stuck' in houses, particularly in the corners (just like cobwebs) and that resonant clapping acts like a kind of sound therapy, dispersing the old energy and leaving the space clear and fresh.

Choose a corner and clap down the wall. So your hands start up high and you clap down, as if you were sending the sound from the ceiling down to the floor. Imagine the noise is clearing away any stuck energy – spiritual debris, if you like. Keep clapping until you notice the sound of your clapping becomes clear. You will know it when it happens – it's quite distinctive. It may only take a few claps or you may need to be persistent if the energy is old and stuck. Now move on to the other corners and progress in this way around your entire home.

BELLING

The next step, in Balinese wisdom, is to put a circle of sound around each room. Walk around the room, ringing a bell in a figure-of-eight movement. This is the symbol of eternity, which tells the energy to go on and on. Choose a bell with a clear, pure sound that appeals to you.

SMUDGING

The origins of smudging are lost in the mists of time, but it's certain that ancient cultures right across the world used the smoke from sacred herbs to protect and cleanse. Originally, it may have been purely practical as our ancestors discovered that driving their livestock through smoke would kill off a host of pests, preventing diseases. Certainly many herbs act as potent pesticides.

Yet the spiritual powers of smoke were also taken very seriously. The Magi didn't just bring gold to the birth of Jesus in the Christian tradition – they also brought frankincense and myrrh, both powerfully protective when burnt as incense. The people of many traditions used incense to inspire them, protect their spaces, and send prayers up to the gods.

Possibly the most well-known is the Native American practice of smudging. The herbs most commonly used are white sage (*Salvia apiana*) and sweetgrass (*Hierochloe odorata*). Sage drives out negative energy – it is a powerful purifier and cleanser. Sweetgrass, on the other hand, is used to attract positive energy.

HOW TO USE A SMUDGE STICK

- Light the end of your stick and let it burn until the tip starts to smoulder. You may need to fan the flames until it catches.
- Waft the stick around your body, sending the smoke up over your head and down to your feet. Smudge your front and back and finish by sending smoke towards your heart.
- Once you feel cleansed, walk around the room you want to smudge, sending smoke up into each corner.
- Stand in the centre of the room. Send out your intention to cleanse the space. Fan smudge out into the East direction. If you wish, you can call on the guardian Spirit Animals. East is guarded by the great Eagle spirit. Imagine those vast wings spreading out to protect the space. Turn to the South and call on the wise Coyote to guard that space. Turn to the West, calling on powerful, protective Bear, and then to the North, summoning the grounding power of Buffalo.
- Send smudge up above you, evoking Father Sky. Then squat to the floor, asking Great Mother Earth to protect the space from below.
- Imagine all these protective forces holding you and your space safe. Put out your stick carefully.

MAKE YOUR SMUDGE STICK

Although smudge sticks are readily available you can make your own, using herbs native to your home.

1. Ideally pick your herbs during the waxing moon. Approach a plant with respect and ask for permission to use it for this sacred purpose.

2. The majority of your smudge stick will need to be made from fresh herbs, but you can include some dried herbs in the middle of your bundle. Use a herb with a sturdy stem as your base. Arrange other stems around it, tucking in any dried herbs.

3. Bind your stick firmly with coloured embroidery thread – but don't use too much cotton. Leave the tip unbound.

4. Hang your stick by the tied end somewhere warm until it is dry.

Herbs to use:

Culinary sage: fosters wisdom and healing.
Lavender: attracts loving energy and creates a peaceful atmosphere.
Cedarwood: deeply purifying; clears negative emotions.
Juniper: purifies, creates safety.
Rosemary: healing; brings clarity.
Yerba Santa: sets and protects boundaries.

MEDICINE WALKING

It's curious that so many of us think of nature as something 'out there'; something we go and visit. We tuck ourselves away in our air-conditioned, centrally-heated homes and watch 'nature' on our television screens or our phones; we follow pretty Instagram accounts; we watch documentaries. If we do go out, we buffer ourselves from the elements – we scuttle to our cars, we tuck ourselves under umbrellas, we hide behind our shades. If we go out into the wild, or even the park, we sit on blankets or chairs. When did you last feel the grass under your bare feet?

Our ancestors would have been so perplexed by the way we separate ourselves from nature. We are nature. We are creatures like any others – we are born, we live, we (some of us) have babies; we die. I'd like to introduce you to a few simple suggestions here to lure you back into your animal skin.

Shamanism is our gateway. Let's walk a little on the medicine path. Shamans look for patterns in the web of life – in the world around us. The shamanic world view says that everything around us can give us knowledge – 'medicine'. Nature, in particular, can give us valuable teachings. The principle has much in common with Jung's idea of synchronicity – meaningful coincidences. Arnold Mindell, founder of Process-oriented psychology, uses something similar when he talks about 'flirts', the things, shapes or colours we notice in our peripheral vision.

Try this when you have a question in your mind, some issue that you'd like guidance on. It doesn't matter where you are – a medicine walk in the city can be as powerful as one in the deep countryside.

Ideally, turn this into a small ritual. Traditionally, you wouldn't eat before your walk, and you would cleanse yourself both physically and energetically. You could have a shower (maybe add a few drops of cedarwood essential oil to your mitt). You might also like to smudge yourself for energetic cleansing.

Make a line of stones outside your front door. You can use small pebbles for this, or even a line of salt. It's a threshold, a liminal space, and by stepping over it, you announce your intention to move into the spirit world.

Step over your line and know that from now on, everything you see or hear or touch will be significant (until you return and step over the line again).

Walk mindfully: feel your feet on the ground beneath you. Notice the world around you – does anything beg for attention? Maybe a bird flies in front of you. You might notice a flower pushing up. You could be drawn to see the ivy clinging to a wall. It might equally be a large bus, people crowding around you or a particular advertisement. Don't worry away at the meaning of what you notice. Just make a mental or physical note and put it aside for pondering later. You can make notes if you like, or take photographs, but don't get too caught up in cerebral stuff – we're exercising our intuitive, spidey-sense muscles here rather than adding to our Insta feed.

When you get home, step back over your threshold, back into 'normal' time and space. Quietly gather up your pebbles. Now it's time to figure out the meaning of your medicine walk. Spend some time quietly meditating on what you discovered. Maybe draw or paint it, or write a poem to it. You can go hunting down the traditional symbolic meanings of, say, swan or fox or oak or ivy (just a few who played with me recently) – or just ponder on what the things that have come to your attention mean to you. Might the ivy suggest you are clinging to something outmoded? What message does the advert give?

You may have brought back some of the items– if so, put them somewhere you can see them in the days to come. An altar is the perfect place.

MAKING ALTARS

An altar is not a big religious deal. They've been part of ancient systems of belief since humans first grasped an inkling of the wonder of the world. They can be totally non-denominational and there really aren't any strict rules.

An altar is simply a place where we can focus our intentions or open ourselves up to the possibility of the divine – something to which we belong. We often make altars quite unconsciously when we place, say, beloved photographs and meaningful items on a mantelpiece. My desk definitely has an altar vibe with a statue of Buddha, crystals, two lucky piskies, favourite quotes and oracle cards, my space diffuser and a scented candle from a dear friend's shop, Eleanor's Byre.

If you're not one of life's natural altar-builders, don't fret. It's simplicity itself. Traditionally an altar would include the following:

- Items which symbolise the elements. So maybe a bowl of water (you could add flowers or petals in the Hindu tradition); a candle (for fire); incense or an aromatherapy burner or diffuser (for air); crystals, stones or a bowl of salt (for earth).

- Images or statues which have meaning for you. They could reflect a faith – a figure of Buddha, Shiva, Durga, the Cross, a Star of David, the Goddess – or they could be secular.

- Items from the natural world – a stone, a piece of wood, a shell, leaves or flowers. This is where you can place anything that you brought back from your medicine walk (pages 76–77).

- Pictures of people dear to you (or, indeed, people you don't like but to whom you are sending love and compassion).

- Often we forget about our own self-care. A picture of yourself – so you can send yourself love and compassion.

- Or, indeed, something that symbolises your goals and aspirations. In feng shui, as we'll discover, it's a good thing to put your life goals out there (life coaches would heartily agree).

SOUND HEALING

Sound healing may be one of the very earliest forms of healing. Some people believe it was used in the mythical lost kingdom of Atlantis. What is clear is that the ancient esoteric schools of India and Tibet, Greece, Egypt and Judaism (to name just a few) all taught the importance of the power of sound. In fact, there is virtually no ancient tradition which does not include sound as a form of healing.

In ancient Greece, healing temples brought about cures by harmonising body and spirit through the power of music. Hinduism, Buddhism and Christianity, to name but a few, have a rich tradition of chants and mantras, while shamanic cultures used drum, bell and rattle to bring about altered states of being.

Now researchers are finding that sound really does affect us on the deepest level. Something that saddens me is that so few of us freely use our voices. It's only really children who still shout and sing for joy. Equally, they'll yell if they're angry and wail if they get hurt. They fully express their emotions for just a short window of time. Once the emotion has been fully released, they can let it go. By the time most people reach their teens, our voices have mainly been silenced. Often we have been shamed, told by teachers or parents that we 'can't sing' or that we're 'tone deaf'.

Stifling our voices not only means that we put a psychological gag on our emotions; it also means we miss out on the many healing powers of sound.

Everything in life has its own frequency. Just try tapping different glasses and you can hear the tone change according to the size, the shape and the thickness of the glass. The opera soprano smashing the glass is simply pitching her voice at the exact frequency of the glass.

Sound healer and researcher Jonathan Goldman believes that every organ, every bone, every cell of the body has its own healthy resonant frequency. Disease is simply part of our body vibrating out of tune. By creating sounds that are harmonious with the 'correct' frequency of the healthy organ, he says we could heal ourselves. It works by 'entrainment', with the healthy sound coaxing the unhealthy element of your body back to its ideal rhythm.

Solfeggio frequencies are a form of hemispheric synchronisation (bringing both sides of the brain into 'whole brain' activity), which dates back to ancient times. They were commonly used in Gregorian chants and other sacred songs. Each Solfeggio tone is comprised of a frequency required to balance energy. There are six main Solfeggio frequencies – ranging from 396Hz (liberating guilt and fear) to 852Hz (returning to spiritual order); 528Hz is known as the 'love' signal, bringing transformation and facilitating DNA repair. This is maybe the easiest introduction to sound healing of all – you just sit back and listen. I'd suggest starting with the stunning chants from Soul Medicine – I play them whenever I'm feeling out of sorts. They have also become part of my bedtime wind-down ritual – I put them on speaker when I'm having my bath and getting ready for sleep.

Being immersed in sound, whether via a gong, singing bowls or drums, is another practice that dates back millennia. Gong baths are a great way to experience sound therapy in a group setting and most people find being bathed in sound a deeply relaxing experience. You simply lie down on a yoga mat, snuggled up in a blanket. The gong player starts quietly and gradually increases the sound of the gong (don't worry – it never gets too loud). You find your mind following the sounds and then, blissfully, you just seem to float off to another level. I think there's something really beautiful about coming together with other people to rest in healing sounds. It's something our ancient ancestors would have done often.

DIY SOUND THERAPY

There are so many ways to use the healing power of sound. You can use your own voice (either alone, with others or singing along to recordings). You can listen to sound (either from voices or instruments). You can feel sound in your body by lying on a sound bed or by feeling the vibrations of voices or instruments near you, as with the gong bath.

- Humming is a wonderful way to calm yourself. If you're feeling anxious or nervous simply hum very gently.
- Exaggerated yawning is the perfect wake-up call and can release tension.
- Deep noisy sighing and groaning can help release irritability or stress. Really let it out!

- Sing whenever you can. Sing along with the radio, while you're driving, or when you're doing chores.
- Tone the different vowel sounds – starting with a deep uuuh and rising up through ooo, oooh, aaah, eeeeh, iiii: Where do you feel them in your body? How do they make you feel?
- Listen to different kinds of music and notice the effect they have on your emotional state. Which types of music relax and soothe you? Which irritate? Which fire you up?
- Experiment with chants and mantras. Even very simple chants can have a pronounced effect on the mind and body. The mind becomes clearer and more relaxed. Om is the simplest chant but also one of the most calming and centring. Check out YouTube for a vast range of chants and mantras. I love Wah! and Deva Premal.
- You can buy a variety of 'singing bowls'. Tibetan, Himalayan, suzu, rin bowls or gongs are all ancient means of making healing sounds – they're believed to date back over 3,000 years. The sides and rim vibrate to make a series of harmonics. Crystal bowls, made of quartz crystal, create beautiful sounds. Also experiment with tuning forks and bells.

HOW SOUND AFFECTS MOOD

Harmonics: Certain kinds of music are rich in harmonics. Gregorian chants, Indian classical music and a cappella singing all change our brain patterns, making us feel more relaxed and connected.

Musical intervals: An interval is created when we play or sing two different notes one after another or at the same time. Some intervals are uplifting (the major third, C/E, and the major fifth, C/G, for example), while minor intervals can make us feel sad. Some intervals are discordant and can induce darker emotions.

Rhythm: Researchers found that listening to Pachelbel's Canon (with a rhythm of 64 beats per minute) changes the brain wave pattern from beta to alpha – 64 beats per minute is the rate of our resting heartbeat. If you want to increase your heart rate, listen to hard-driving rock music. If you want to lower it, take the pace right down.

Drumming: Repetitive drumming can take you into a trance-like state. The regular beat of the drum entrains the heartbeat to its rhythm, so you can gradually slow the drum to reduce the heartbeat and breathing rate.

SUMMER

INTRODUCTION

Summer comes in with a lazy, well-fed smile. The sun bestows a blessing, hearts lift, minds relax and bodies sigh with pleasure. For our ancestors, summer would have ushered in a time of relative ease as they no longer needed to battle against the cold and damp. However, it was no picnic either – tending crops was tough work, but everything seems easier when the regenerative sun is shining.

Summer is the culmination of the thrusting yang energy of spring. Wood has burned into the 'full yang' of fire. It's not hard to see how summer is the most energetic phase of the year's wheel – yang energy grows and spreads, thanks to that powerful fire of the sun.

Fire governs the heart and the small intestine, so these are the major organs and meridians of the season. Every ancient system teaches that the heart is the seat of our emotions, above all related to feelings of love and joy, generosity and compassion, abundance, openness and, of course, warmth. The small intestine is key to digestion – it connects the stomach and the large intestine and is divided into three sections – the duodenum, the jejunum and the ileum. Sadly, it's all too easy for this precious pathway to become clogged, blocked or leaky.

If you have imbalances around the heart meridian or Anahata, the heart chakra (see page 100), they will often manifest as anxiety, fear, palpitations, sadness and yearning. If heart energy is blocked, it's also common to see people suffering from problems with their circulation and hypertension.

When the small intestine meridian is out of balance, we often become insecure and vulnerable. We have a sense of feeling lost, so anything and everything can become a struggle. The 'evil' of summer is, unsurprisingly, heat (or, more correctly, overheating). It's wonderful to open ourselves to the sun, but we all know the dangers of too many rays. Everyone and, in particular, those with a pitta constitution, should take care not to overheat and burn.

Our focus on diet over the hot summer months is about keeping our bodies cool and balanced. It's also a good time to investigate fermented foods – a new trend that harks back to a very ancient tradition.

Our yoga practice changes again to welcome in the big ease of summer. Warm bodies stretch far more easily and we'll honour that, while working with the key summer meridians in a gentle, grounding version of that old favourite – the Sun Salutation.

Summer holidays put us in mind of the seaside, but you don't have to go to the beach to enjoy some delicious water cures – we'll make a splash in this section, indulging in some venerable hydrotherapy.

Native American tradition sees summer as a time to widen our perceptions, to become far more aware of how we express love, both to ourselves and to other people. It's the natural time to explore our emotional wellbeing so we'll be looking at how we can use bodywork as a means of freeing emotion caught in our physiology. We'll also look at simple ways of bringing joy into our lives, and understanding the lessons of sadness and 'negative' emotions. It's a good time to look at our relationship to our sexuality and sensuous nature too.

Our spirits open and relax in these months so we'll dive into some truly lovely ancient healing practices – from colour therapy to chakra healing. We'll walk in forests and lie out under the moon to dream. It's summer – and for sure the living can be easy.

SUMMER DIET

All the ancient traditions agree that this is the time to introduce lighter, cooler foods into your diet. Fire energy rises with the sun and it can easily become imbalanced, causing indigestion and stress.

So the rule of thumb during a hot summer is – keep your cool. On the whole you're looking at colder, sweeter, softer foods and cool drinks (the exception to this is anyone who's strongly vata in their constitution, in which case keep to lightly warmed foods and drinks).

Neither Ayurveda nor TCM is too keen on cold food; however this is the one time of year that raw and cool can be best tolerated by the body. The only slight problem is that they can tend to dampen down 'agni', the digestive fire – so balance your cold soups, salads and ice creams with warmer foods (or take a little ginger tea before you eat them).

Equally, too much hot spicy food at this time can bring headaches and biliousness that might stretch right through until autumn.

Keep your meat intake down during summer. Yes, it's barbecue season and some grilled meat won't hurt once in a while, but think about alternatives – grilled fish, vegetable kebabs, grilled tofu or veggie burgers. Halloumi works a treat on the griddle. Just try to steer clear of red meat and, in particular, highly processed meat. Also make sure you don't burn your barbecued food – nobody wants to be a killjoy but burnt food is recognised as a serious health risk.

Also, keeping on with that party pooper mood, try to keep your alcohol intake down in summer – it really can aggravate that fire energy. There are masses of soft drink options – you're spoilt for choice with all those fruit shrubs, flavoured kombucha and kefir (also gut-friendly), and infused botanicals. If alcohol is non-negotiable, water it down: white wine spritzers, gin with loads of tonic, low gravity beers and lagers.

So, let's look in more detail at our fire-reducing diet for summer. As you might expect, there's a glut of vegetables and fruits you can eat now. In fact, it's easier to say what's not so good to eat. If we're going to keep to strict Ayurvedic guidelines, we would go easy on sour fruits (sour apples and sour cherries, cranberries, plums, green grapes and rhubarb) at this time of year. The sweet versions of these are absolutely fine. Also, take it easy with pungent vegetables – that's onions, tomatoes, pumpkin, radish, turnips and cooked leeks – all too heating for the body. However, it's open season on sweet and bitter vegetables, such as cauliflower, leafy greens, salad greens, mushrooms, potatoes, sprouts, courgettes, asparagus, artichokes and so on.

Grain-wise, you should focus on barley, cooked oats and rice. If you're not intolerant of wheat, now's the time to eat it. If it gives you problems, it might be worth trying sourdough – the ancient method of proving and cooking sourdough makes it far more easily digestible.

This is a great time of year for indulging in legumes of all sorts – the only outsiders in summer are black and red lentils (too warming). Enjoy tofu hot and cold, and add in tempeh and other soy products too.

Coconut is your go-to nut and oil for summer. It has a profoundly cooling effect and is a friend in need to pitta types all year round. Ghee is also fine. Most people can tolerate a little dairy in the summer (providing it doesn't cause you issues) – but think of mild soft cheeses and cottage cheese in particular. Pumpkin and sunflower seeds are delicious dry-roasted and added to salads, Bircher muesli and porridge.

Herbs and spices should be lighter and more fragrant. Add basil, mint (garden mint, spearmint, peppermint), parsley, and fennel freely to your food. (If you don't already, maybe think about growing them in your garden or in window boxes.) Dill promotes digestion and can soothe sickness and stomach ache. It can help painful periods and can soothe slight fevers. Turmeric, cardamom, cinnamon, cumin, neem and saffron are your go-to spices. Vanilla is the sweet flavouring for summer. Coriander is considered to be sweet, bitter, astringent and pungent – so it is very useful for cooling fevers and great for adding to dishes and drinks in the heat of summer (use the leaves and the seeds). It strengthens the nerves and the brain.

Fermented foods and drinks are really enjoying 'a moment' as modern sensibilities catch up with ancient wisdom. When we say ancient here we're talking seriously ancient – the earliest recorded use of fermentation dates right back to 6,000 BCE. Nearly every culture boasts at least one fermented food – from the familiar chutneys of India, the kimchi of Korea and the sauerkraut of middle and Eastern Europe to lesser known foods like the Tanzanian togwa and West African garri. Foods were initially fermented as a means of preservation, but the links between fermented food and health swiftly became apparent. Now, of course, we know that certain probiotics (beneficial bacteria) help balance the biome, supporting our immune systems and affecting pretty much every part of the body. So, if you haven't already discovered the joy of fermentation, now's the ideal time to start.

If you love smoothies, this is the time of year to indulge. It's also fine to drink your fill of juices and shakes. Just take a little protein with any sweet drinks that don't already contain it – so, maybe a handful of seeds or a couple of walnuts or almonds. Why? Protein helps to balance blood sugar, which could be elevated by the fruit.

HERBAL TEAS AND WATERS

The ancients loved warm drinks, even in summer. Herbal teas really come into their own now and make delightfully refreshing drinks. If you have a garden, or window box, you can use fresh leaves: try nettle, lemon balm, mint, spearmint, dandelion, borage, chamomile, fennel, elderflower and lavender. Ideally pick the buds or leaves in the early morning and gently wash them. Experiment with your own blends. Keep well hydrated. It's always important but even more so in the summer. One nice way of making water more interesting is to add some fresh leaves or fruit to a carafe. Lemon, mint, cucumber and rosemary all work well but really, just use your imagination.

SUMMER YOGA

As we've already seen, the meridians associated with summer and the fire element are those of the heart and the small intestine. These particular meridians run up and down and through the arms, up into the head, and across into the chest and centre of your body.

So we will focus on opening the chest area, extending and reaching with our arms, allowing our awareness to travel to the tips of the fingers and beyond. Working both with your body and with the breath, you'll bring vital energy directly to these meridians, bringing them into balance. A gentle and simple way to inspire this rebalancing is a form of mini Sun Salutation (Surya Namaskar). Start by kneeling rather than standing as starting closer to the earth will conserve your vulnerable energy. Later, as your energy comes into better balance, you can move into the standing form. Take this nice and slowly – it's not a race. Focus on moving your body with the breath, allowing your inhale and exhale to lead the movement. Eventually you will find you can flow smoothly from one pose to another. Just do your best while visualising yourself doing the perfect movement. Research shows that, incredibly, mentally imaging the moves has nearly the same effect as the movements themselves.

1. Kneel on a cushioned mat. Sit back on your heels with your hands in Prayer pose (Pranamasana) over your heart.

2. Draw in a deep invigorating breath to start, allowing the heart to open and fire up the belly at the same time. Reach upwards to the sky, straightening your body at the same time. Reach up and out with joy.

3. Breathing out, gently come onto your hands and knees, keeping your body square (hands over shoulders, knees over hips).

4. Breathing in, arch your back to the sky like a cat (Cat pose – Marjaryasana).

5. Breathing out, softly allow your back to dip towards the earth (Cow pose – Bitilasana).

6. Breathing in, lower and slide your head and upper body down between your hands into Cobra pose (Bhujangasana). As your arms bend and take your weight, you may need to keep your elbows close in to the ribs in order to generate the strength to land smoothly on the mat. Gently push into the ground with your hands to arch the upper body, upwards and backwards (don't overstretch).

7. Breathing out, push into the ground with your hands and take your bottom backwards to connect with your heels, into Child's pose (Balasana). Your arms are stretched forwards in front of you.

8. Breathing in, smoothly roll up your spine, vertebra by vertebra, bringing your arms out into a wide arc before you pull them back to Prayer position in front of your dear heart.

9. You are back in your original position. You can repeat the whole salutation. Three full repetitions would be ideal.

THE COOLING BREATH

Let's finish our yoga practice with the Cooling Breath (Sitali). The name really does say it all and this breathing technique works brilliantly when we feel overwhelmed by the heat.

1. Sit comfortably, ideally with a gentle lift up through the spine. To help this, pull your buttock cheeks backwards, so you're sitting on your tailbone. Perching on the edge of a cushion or bolster can help align your spine.

2. Now roll your tongue into a tube and simply breathe slowly and calmly through your mouth. Your breath is cooled by the moisture in your mouth before it reaches your windpipe. This brings down your inner temperature and also soothes the stress response, switching on the parasympathetic nervous system.
Note: Some people are not genetically wired to be able to curl their tongues. If you're one of them, you can still enjoy this breath. Simply keep your mouth slightly open and draw in air over your tongue.

WATER
SUMMER'S CURE FOR HEAT

As we've seen, summer is full-on yang energy. We're already soothing that fire with foods that have more of a cooling yin quality. However, we can also use water, the most yin of all the elements. Water is flowing, receptive, adaptive – put it in a container and it will spread to fit.

Temperature is all. This isn't the time of year generally for hot baths or steaming saunas – we'll save those for winter. However, it is the perfect time to indulge in wild swimming. Swimming pools are all fine and good but nothing beats the refreshment of river, lake or sea bathing. Yes, it can be a bit messy and muddy. No, there aren't showers and changing rooms on tap. So what? Unleash your inner wild woman or man and get at one with nature. I'm a lacklustre swimmer but it doesn't put me off. I just make sure I don't go beyond my limits. While my swimming is rubbish, I love floating. Truly, there is nothing more lovely than lying back in the water and watching the clouds or the stars. Pure heaven.

The healing power of water, known as hydrotherapy, has a long and venerable history, and now science is finding out exactly why. Immersion in cool or cold water can decrease blood pressure, improve circulation, decrease levels of stress hormones and boost levels of happy hormones, soothe inflammation, and help kick depression into touch. Not bad for a dip.

If you're not up for wild swimming, you can gain many of the benefits in the comfort of your own bathroom. Simply finishing off your shower with a blast of cold water will give you a natural boost. Or try a soothing bath from the old European tradition of naturopathy.

APPLE CIDER VINEGAR BATH

This is the perfect soothing summer bath. It is the ideal pick-me-up if you're feeling jaded by the heat, and can also help soothe sunburned or itchy skin. However, it is not suitable for anyone with high blood pressure or a heart condition. Use organic apple cider vinegar (the type labelled 'with the mother') if you can for best results.

- Firstly splash apple cider vinegar all over your body.
- Add a cup of vinegar to a warm (but not baking hot) bath. Soak for 10 minutes or so.

DREAMY SUMMERTIME BATH

This takes a bit of effort but it really is a dreamy summertime bath. It's based on the old European herbal tradition, using herbs that all have stellar reputations for easing you into deep relaxation.

- Take 3 tablespoons each of the following fresh or dried herbs – chamomile, cowslip, woodruff, vervain and linden blossom.
- Simmer them for about 20 minutes in 3 litres water.
- Draw a warm bath (it shouldn't be too hot) and strain the herbal decoction through a piece of muslin into the bath.
- Tie up the muslin with the herbs into a bag.
- Add 4 drops of Roman chamomile essential oil to the water and swish it around to disperse. You can use lavender if you prefer.
- Use your herbal bag as a flannel and relax in the water.

COOLING ESSENTIAL OILS FOR SUMMER

You can add any of these oils to your bath for a refreshing and sweet-smelling cooler. Add a few drops of your chosen oils to a cup of milk or a few tablespoons of a carrier oil (sweet almond and coconut are both great summer choices). Gently mix them together and swirl into a warm bath. Once you find a blend you like, you can also use it for massage or to dab on your temples and wrists during hot summer days.

- Peppermint, spearmint
- Lavender
- Sandalwood
- Vetiver
- Lemon
- Lemongrass
- Bergamot
- German or Roman chamomile

BODYWORK FOR FREEING EMOTIONS

Our ancient forebears discovered that touch, massage and pressure didn't just affect our bodies on a physiological level – they also affected our emotions. It was understood that our bodies acted like a library of our lives, storing our entire history. So all our memories, our hurts, fears and traumas (as well as our joys and triumphs) were not just retained in our brains but enmeshed throughout the entire body – in our muscles, tendons, fascia; even in our organs and our very bones. Yes, the subconscious is actually spread right throughout our physical being.

By working with the body, a skilled therapist can dissolve the stuck chemistry we carry. How? It seems that, particularly during periods of trauma, we make snapshots of experiences that carry high levels of emotional content. It's as if our body realises that they're too painful for our conscious minds, so it wraps them up and keeps them deeply hidden as a form of protective mechanism. This can be a good thing in the direct aftermath of a bad experience but, as time goes on, those repressed memories can result in both psychological issues (such as guilt, anxiety, fear, shame, anger) and also physiological pain and discomfort.

In particular, it's our fascia (the connective tissue) that adapts to hold old pain. It is well known that fascia will adapt to protect a physical injury, but what isn't so well known is that it will also hunch around an emotional hurt, locking it deep in the body. However,

fascia is malleable and if it is stretched and manipulated back to its ideal position, the neurological pathways can be reprogrammed. When the body changes on a physiological level, it often changes on an emotional level too.

The beauty of bodywork is that you don't need to talk. Your therapist won't ask you to delve deep into your past or to confront painful memories. It is said that the body has a wisdom of its own and that it will choose the time to release held energy and suppressed emotions. So this can be a tender, gentle, kind way to heal your emotional wellbeing. However, do be aware that your bodyworker may not also be a trained psychotherapist. You may well find that the best way to work is with talking and body therapies working in tandem.

Many of the bodywork therapies we talk about in this book may well bring about emotional release.

GETTING IN TOUCH WITH THE BODY

You can start the process by becoming gently aware of your body. Often we will go through an entire day without actually checking in and finding out how our bodies are doing.

- **Paying attention:** Lie on the floor, ideally on a yoga mat. Feel the mat underneath you, notice where it supports your body. Now bring attention to your feet – visualise the bones, the muscles, the ligaments, the tendons, the skin. Is there any difference between each foot? Gradually work your way up your body, checking in as you go.
- **Bone tapping:** Lightly clench your fists and swiftly and gently tap over your hip-bones and pelvis. What sound do they make? Where do you feel the vibration in your body? Now tap down your legs and notice the difference. Experiment with other areas of your body.

- **Heart matters:** Sit quietly and listen to the sound of your heart. Bring your focus right inside it and hear its rhythm. Imagine you are breathing from your heart. Now, if this feels okay, go deeply within the heart – listen to the blood as it moves through the valves. How do you feel?
- **Deep body love:** This is an exercise from the Hawaiian Kahuna tradition. Take off your clothes and sit or stand in front of a full-length mirror. Resist the urge to berate your body – find a part you like. It might be tiny – just your fingertips – but that's a start. Keep looking. Are your earlobes okay? Think of the amazing job your fingertips do, and your ears. Just sit quietly, reaffirming the miracle that is your body. Emotions may well arise and that's fine.

If you feel overwhelmed, seek the help of a professional therapist. It's good work, but you may need an extra helping hand.

COLOUR THERAPY

Some imaginative souls say that the history of colour therapy stretches right back to the mythical culture of Atlantis. Sick people were placed in healing rooms constructed of crystals angled so the sunlight would diffuse through them to give beams of rainbow light. The healing temples of ancient Greece knew of the therapeutic value of colour and in ancient Egypt there were temples known as the healing temples of light and colour. The healing traditions of India and China testify to the power of different colours to heal both physically and psychologically.

It makes sense. Our whole bodies are sensitive to colour. Russian research has found that many people can be trained to detect colour with their fingertips, possibly by picking up on the unique vibrational frequency of each colour. Other research shows that colour can affect everything from health to happiness, from success to our sex lives. Red walls in a pub could mean more fights at closing time. Pink walls in a prison make inmates quieter, while royal blue in a custody cell encourages people to come clean and tell the truth.

Literally seeing red can stimulate the glandular system and increase the heart rate, blood pressure and respiration. Patients with high blood pressure have been shown to lower their blood pressure on demand simply by visualising the colour blue.

Ideally we should give ourselves a broad spectrum of colour. If your problems involve coldness, poor circulation, lethargy or constipation,

concentrate on the warmer colours – reds, oranges, yellows and pinks. If you are feverish or suffer from inflammation and 'hot' conditions, the soothing blue and green shades could cool you down.

COLOUR BREATHING

Choose the colour you feel is most needed in your life. Now sit or lie down and breathe in a relaxed, easy manner. Imagine yourself bathed in your chosen colour. As you breathe in, visualise the colour coming into your body via your solar plexus (just above your navel). The colour spreads throughout your entire body. As you breathe out, imagine the complementary colour suffusing and leaving your body. Repeat for at least 10 rounds, or for as long as you like.

BRINGING COLOUR INTO YOUR LIFE

There are many ways of using colour. Try wearing clothes in the colour you think you need, or introduce different colours into your home décor.

Red: increases your energy and vitality, and can also fire up your sexuality. It's good for confidence too – adding red to an outfit (even just a scarf or tie) can have a noticeable effect. However, go easy with red in the home, as it can be overstimulating in large amounts. The complementary colour to red is turquoise.

Orange: creates fun, happiness and joy. Softer hues work well in sociable spaces, such as living rooms. Its complement is blue.

Yellow: helps concentration, stimulates the intellect and increases your ability to be objective. It's an ideal colour for offices and home studies. Its complement is violet.

Green: the great balancer, cleanser and healer. The colour of nature, it is supremely restful for the human psyche. Use it to keep yourself in balance. In soft tones it's ideal for any room in the home. Its complement is magenta.

Blue: relaxes and brings peace to body and mind. It's the colour to visualise if you feel stressed or can't sleep and when you need to think calmly and rationally. It's a great colour for offices and also bedrooms. Its complement is orange.

Violet: the colour of dignity and self-respect. It promotes self-esteem, so add a dash of violet when you feel overwhelmed or not up to a task. Its complement is yellow.

Magenta: the great releaser. Used in colour therapy for helping to release old thoughts and obsessions. It's a very spiritual colour so, in softer tones, perfect for meditation rooms. Its complement is green.

CHAKRA HEALING

Ancient Eastern wisdom teaches that there are certain places in the human body where vital energy comes together. Visualised as spinning spheres of energy, vibrating at different frequencies, these are the chakras. The seven most important ones run in a line from the base of the spine to the crown of the head.

SAHASRARA
the Crown Chakra

AJNA
the Brow Chakra

VISHUDDHA
the Throat Chakra

ANAHATA
the Heart Chakra

MANIPURA
the Solar Plexus Chakra

SVADISTHANA
the Sacral Chakra

MULADHARA
the Root Chakra

When each chakra spins at its perfect frequency our bodies radiate perfect health, our minds are calm and our emotions balanced. Yet, we all too easily fall out of balance and our chakras spin out of sync. Imagine them as a radio – the sound is muddy and crackly until you hit exactly the right wavelength when everything suddenly becomes crystal clear.

It's actually quite easy to tell which of your chakras are out of balance. Equally there are some simple life shifts you can make to help them come back into equilibrium. Let's have a look.

MULADHARA -

the Base or Root Chakra

This chakra is situated at the base of the spine. Its colour is red. Muladhara governs the material world, our physical structure, our sense of safety and survival. When it is balanced, we have good levels of energy and feel safe and solid in our world.

Effects of imbalance: If this chakra is lacking in energy, you may feel out of connection with your body. You could suffer from anxiety and restlessness, find it hard to focus and be very disorganised. If you have too much energy here, you may overeat and be overweight. Sluggishness, laziness and low energy levels are common side effects.

On a physical level, imbalance in this chakra can affect your bones, teeth, intestines and bowels. Areas of weakness also include the lower part of the body, from the base of the spine down.

How to balance Muladhara: Make friends with your body. Bodywork really helps forge a connection here and slow focused yoga practices, such as Yin yoga or Kundalini yoga can help you feel grounded, as can qigong (see page 169). Try gardening and pottery, or baking your own bread. On the emotional level, look at your early relationship with your mother – it may need healing work.

SVADISTHANA –
the Sacral Chakra

This chakra is located below the navel. Its colour is orange. Svadisthana governs our sexuality and relationships. When it's in balance we are able to enjoy our bodies without guilt or shame. We have a grace about our movements and our emotions are balanced. We are kind to ourselves and to other people.

Effects of imbalance: If this chakra is low in energy you may feel a lack of desire, passion and excitement in life. Your libido may be sluggish or nonexistent. You could have a fear of change and a denial of pleasure. If its energy is excessive, you could be addicted to pleasure and sex. Your mood might swing unpredictably and you could find yourself lurching from crisis to crisis. Oversensitivity and an overdependence on other people are common. Imbalance could be flagged up by problems in the reproductive and urinary systems. You could experience lack of flexibility in the lower back and knees, and sexual dysfunction.

How to balance Svadisthana: Bring awareness to all your senses – try different foods; feel the textures around you; dive into nature and art; listen to all kinds of music. Dance is wonderful for liberating this chakra. On an emotional level, you may need to release old feelings of hurt, anger and guilt – particularly around sex and sexuality.

MANIPURA –
the Solar Plexus Chakra

This chakra is found at the solar plexus, the upper part of the abdomen around the diaphragm. Its colour is yellow. When Manipura is balanced you feel pretty good – full of healthy self-esteem and a warm sense of confidence. You have a well-developed sense of humour, can meet challenges and are responsible and reliable. Spontaneity and playfulness are part of your sunny disposition.

Effects of imbalance: If you're low in energy and your self-esteem is rocky, you could be low in energy here. Likewise, if you find yourself easily becoming the victim, blaming others and the world for your problems, look to Manipura. If your Manipura energy is on the excessive side, you could be domineering, manipulative, overly competitive and stubborn.

Problems with digestion are common when Manipura is unbalanced. You may also have issues with the stomach, pancreas, gall bladder and liver.

How to balance Manipura: Strengthening your core can help this chakra so look to yoga and Pilates. Martial arts are excellent. Psychotherapy can help you strengthen your sense of balanced autonomy. If you have a deficiency here, you need grounding and emotional warmth above all. If it's excessive, then look at deep relaxation.

ANAHATA -
the Heart Chakra

As you might expect, the heart chakra is found in the area of the heart and chest. Its colour is green. Its focus is issues of love, balance, relationships and intimacy. When it's spinning in balance, it makes you compassionate, loving, peaceable and altruistic. You feel warmth towards people and have empathy towards their problems.

Effects of imbalance: Too little energy here and you will tend to feel withdrawn, maybe antisocial, critical and judgemental. You may also suffer from depression, loneliness and a fear of relationships. Too much energy in the this chakra brings jealousy and/or dependency. You could be demanding or clinging.

On a physical level, imbalance may cause disorders of the heart, lungs, breasts and arms. Asthma, circulation problems, immune system deficiency and shoulder tension may be common.

How to balance Anahata: Breathing is your major ally. Focus on the pranayama exercises in this book or discover more online or in a class. Check out deep breathwork practices such as Transformational Breath or Holotropic Breathwork®. Journaling is also a good tool – write down all your feelings. Suppressed grief and loss can be issues here – work with a therapist if necessary.

VISHUDDHA -
the Throat Chakra

This chakra is located in the throat. Its colour is clear blue. It focuses on communication and creativity. When balanced you have a great sense of timing and rhythm. Your voice will be clear and confident – you aren't scared of speaking out, of speaking your truth. You are a good communicator and also have a strong sense of creativity in your life.

Effects of imbalance: If you're scared of speaking out, hate the sound of your own voice or struggle to communicate clearly, you may be deficient in this chakra. Introversion and shyness are common. If, on the other hand, you have too much energy here, you could be a bit of a loudmouth, someone who talks too much and listens too little or too poorly. Gossiping, interrupting and speaking over people are clear signs. Physical signs of imbalance include disorders of the throat, ears, neck and voice.

How to balance Vishuddha: if you're lacking in energy here, you need to use your voice. Try singing, chanting, humming; even yelling maybe. Often there is energy stuck and expressing your grief or rage can be nigh on miraculous for healing it. Investigate sound therapy. If there's too much energy here, try silence (maybe even a silent retreat). Make yourself focus on listening, really listening.

AJNA -
the Brow or Third-Eye Chakra

The sixth chakra is located between the eyebrows on the forehead. Its colour is indigo and its realm is the imagination, intuition, dreams and insights. When it's balanced you will be perceptive and have a developed sense of intuition. You find it easy to use your imagination.

Effects of imbalance: Too little energy here and you will lack imagination and intuition. You may suffer from poor memory, find it hard to remember your dreams and struggle to visualise the future. Your thinking could be rigid and controlled. If, on the other hand, your brow chakra is low in energy, you could find it hard to concentrate. You could be obsessive and might have bad nightmares.

Physical signs of imbalance include frequent headaches, poor eyesight or other vision problems.

How to balance Ajna: Work with non-rational forms of creativity – art therapy is wonderful here, not focusing on painting pretty pictures but letting your unconscious take over the paint. Working with your dreams (see page 178) will also help. Meditation is another boon here.

SAHASRARA -
the Crown Chakra

The seventh chakra is found in the cerebral cortex of the brain, right at the crown of the head. Its colour is violet and it provides our connection with the wider energy of consciousness and the divine. When Sahasrara is in balance, you are open-minded, thoughtful and wise. You can easily assimilate information and make connections. Most likely you have a balanced spiritual life.

Effects of imbalance: Lack of energy in this chakra tends to make you cynical, greedy and materialistic. Too much energy here and you're likely to live solely in your head – you may feel spacey and out of touch with your body. Ungrounded spirituality manifests in this way.

Migraine and amnesia are physical effects here.

How to balance Sahasrara: Embodied meditation is very useful here. Always be open to new ideas and information – combat rigidity of thought. If you have excessive energy here, ground yourself with strong bodywork, qigong, or gardening. If there's too little, allow yourself to release cynicism just a little – try keeping an open mind.

SHINRIN-YOKU - FOREST BATHING

Purists would argue that shinrin-yoku (which translates as 'forest bathing') is actually a pretty modern concept – it was formalised in Japan in the 1980s. However, I think we'd all agree it is something we've been doing all by ourselves since primeval times.

Buddhism, Shintoism, Shamanism and many other ancient systems of belief saw forests (as well as other forms of nature) as mystical, spiritual and deeply healing for the human soul. Shamanism sees spirits in the rocks, in the trees, in every part of the landscape, and forests were often a place of initiation, a place of learning.

Now modern research shows that trees really do have healing powers quite outside their natural majesty and beauty. Going into the woods can help boost your immune system, and lower your blood pressure, heart rate and stress hormones. It's been shown to increase energy and good mood, while reducing anxiety, depression and anger. When we are in nature, our brains behave differently, so connecting with nature is actually a process of resetting your brain – switching off that flight/fight/freeze response (associated with the sympathetic nervous system) and allowing us to sink into the healing rest and repair response of the parasympathetic system.

One precise way trees heal us is by the release of antimicrobial essential oils (known as phytoncides). The trees use them for pest control but they benefit us humans too, in all the ways listed above.

However, I think it's more than that. When we're in the woods (or, equally, on top of a mountain or by the ocean or on the high moors) we feel a kinship, a knowing, a return to an older, simpler, much healthier symbiosis. Evolutionary biologist Edward O Wilson called this 'biophilia' (loving life), recognising that, as part of creation, we have a deep urge to commune with our Mother Earth. Cities are fun, vibrant, exciting – but our souls sink deep in nature. We were designed to drink in the wild outdoors.

University of Michigan psychologist Stephen Kaplan says that, when we go into the woods, we enter a state of, 'soft fascination'. Our minds aren't struggling to process the relentless onslaught of stimuli so we're able to let our attention be captured gently by the wonders around us.

All it really takes is you and a bit of woodland. Don't route march your way through your wood – this isn't a hike.

- Meander, go slow; take the time to wander. See what catches your eye, or your nose, or your feet (if you can go barefoot, so much the better).
- Is one particular tree calling to you? I once spent several years communing with a young oak in a nearby wood. I can honestly say that tree became as dear to me as any friend. Yes, hug your tree too. In fact, hug lots of trees. I used to lean back against my tree, feeling his (yes, I think he was a he) strength and solid timeless love.
- Sit down maybe, close your eyes and listen. Really listen. What can you hear? The more you do this, the longer you do this, the more you will notice. The forest may seem silent but really there's a symphony going on.
- Breathe deeply. Really suck in those healing phytoncides. Trees all have different phytoncides with varying properties. D-limonene, for example, purportedly works better than antidepressants. Sniff the earth too.
- Feeling peckish? If you know what you're doing, you can eat the forest too. I have happy memories of forest bathing with my friend Kate who knows what's what. We nibbled whortleberries and picked mushrooms to take home to cook (the taste was out of this world). You can also bring a flask of tea (maybe made from berries or leaves picked on a previous trip). Sip, savour.

MOONBATHING

We've been worshipping the moon for millennia and summer is the perfect time to catch those moon rays. Moon worship spans ancient religions across the world – from India, China, Africa, the Middle East, the Americas and Europe. It's believed to precede worship of the sun in every ancient culture. Although we often tend to associate moon worship with goddesses (such as Chinese Chang'e, Greek Selene, Egyptian Isis, or Roman Luna, for example) there are equally as many lunar gods (Babylonian Sin, Japanese Tsukuyomi, Indian Chandra, to name a few).

Many ancient cultures developed a lunar calendar – and the moon still rules over festivals in the Hindu, Jewish, Taoist, Buddhist and even, in the case of Easter, Christian faiths. The moon was our first calendar and many cultures (including Native American, Irish and West African) give names to the thirteen full moons that usually make up the solar year.

Moonbathing is used to cool those with too much pitta fire energy in Ayurveda. It's said to help calm hypertension, hives, rashes and other inflammatory conditions. However, during high summer, everyone can benefit from its soothing, cooling light. Ideally, moonbathe during the waxing phase of the moon. The full moon is considered the most auspicious time of all.

MOON MEDITATION

In many cultures, the full moon is a time to meditate, to step outside normal everyday life and focus on the ineffable. Buddhists celebrate full-moon days because of the auspicious events that happened to Buddha. Why not follow the Buddhist way and set aside some time in meditation or contemplation on full-moon days. Using the moon as a meditation symbol is supposed to take you into a deeper state of meditation.

If you are a crystal lover, this is also the perfect time to cleanse your crystals. Wash them gently, then lay them out under the rays of our heavenly neighbour.

LUNAR TEA

Brew up some lunar tea to capture the essence of the moon. Choose your favourite herbs and edible flowers – rose, lavender, lemon balm and borage; throw in some catnip, passionflower, hibiscus and violet leaves – it's a moveable feast. Place the washed flowers and leaves in a glass or crystal container. Pour cold water (ideally spring water) over the herbs so that they're totally immersed. Let it sit outside in full view of the moon. Come morning, simply strain and enjoy.

LATE
SUMMER

INTRODUCTION

In the Chinese Five Element system, late summer is a season all of its own. It's seen as the fulcrum of the year, a time of perfect balance that contains elements of all the seasons. It's an in-between period, when the fire of summer mellows into the balanced energy of earth. Neither yin nor yang holds sway here. Ayurveda also sees this as a pivotal time when all the elements of the body can be disturbed.

The element here is earth, central to all the other elements. The colour is yellow – that of the sun and earth combined. Its direction is the centre. Earth holds sway over the stomach and the spleen (plus the pancreas). If you have unbalanced earth in your system, it's highly likely your stomach will tell you about it.

This is a particularly tricky seasonal shift and all ancient wisdom stresses how important it is to keep ourselves balanced and centred. However, it's also an exciting time, giving the possibilities of new beginnings, thoughts, views and opinions. Fire energy moving into earth gives the possibility to shake things up and kick-start new ways of living. Just watch out that your enthusiasm doesn't tip over into

obsession. This transitional time can flag up any stubbornness or obsessiveness in your personality. Be aware of becoming a tad dictatorial – insisting you're right and everyone else is wrong.

On the physical front, imbalances in earth energy can cause issues with your menstrual cycle and your digestion. The spleen, so often overlooked, comes into play now as well. This organ supposedly governs memory, willpower and our ability to form opinions. Any deficiency here can lead to poor decision making, forgetfulness and possibly even anxiety.

Late summer can have a humid damp quality as autumn approaches. It may even be a monsoon time depending on where you live. As both the stomach and spleen are considered to be damp organs, keeping balance can be more tricky if there is a lot of water around. Any imbalance in the spleen can create cravings for sweet things and can lead to weight gain.

It's also supposed to be a time of sympathy and empathy. A motherly nurturing quality can emerge, so notice any imbalances between our own and others' needs. Can we hold the space for both? Can we care for others without losing sight of our own needs?

Make sure you're well-grounded and nourished, both physically and emotionally. Just be aware that issues around self-esteem and trust can come up at this time of year. You may notice a lack of identity and healthy psychological boundaries. We need to feel the support of Mother Earth, to accept that we all need to be held, no matter how strong we may think we are. If we tune in, we will find the encouragement to strengthen our sense of self-worth and find our own stability. Then, and only then, are we in a position to give support to others.

At this time of year it's useful to spend time thinking how we can let our needs be met from within. What really nourishes you? What do you need in order to feel good?

Many of us think we have to go it alone; that being strong means that we mustn't rely on other people for support. Try to challenge that thought if it applies to you. Reach out in a way that feels safe and appropriate. Find groups of like-minded people – often it can be easier to open up to strangers than to friends. Ancient cultures rarely leave people on their own to stew – they gather together to talk, to share, to figure out what's going on. Sobonfu Somé, the great authority on African spirituality, famously said: 'There is a deep longing among people in the West to connect with something bigger – with community and spirit.'

Think about approaches that will help you centre yourself – try writing, painting or dancing as a way of balancing.

Our yoga practice will help balance the key meridians and we're also going to look at yoga for our hands, the wonderful art of mudras. Mudras are gestures that create a circuit in our bodies, channelling vital energy in specific ways.

One of the best ways of keeping ourselves on an even keel is, I believe, switching our focus to others. It's all too easy in this crazy modern world to adopt a 'fortress me' mentality. If we extend our practice out to other people, it has the curious effect of healing ourselves as well. So I'm going to introduce you to a Hawaiian tradition. We'll end with some gentle emotional healing from the most beautiful source – flowers.

LATE SUMMER DIET

This is the time to start a building and toning diet in readiness for the cooler weather to come. Enjoy all the rich variety of fruits and vegetables available now – this really is a time when nature overwhelms with its bounty.

I always associate watermelon with this time of year and, if the weather is still warm, it's a good time for a short watermelon cleanse. Simply substitute watermelon juice for one of your meals a day (munch a few nuts or seeds to offset the sugar rush).

You can also try making a tea from watermelon seeds. The seeds are a great source of glutathione, the natural antioxidant which protects pretty much all our bodies from oxidative damage. To make the tea, crush around a cup of watermelon seeds and boil them in 1 litre of water for around 5 minutes.

Cool, strain and keep in the fridge.

Sweet round vegetables come into their own right now – think cabbage, onions, pumpkin, turnips, swedes. Sea vegetables add interest – miso soup with kombu is light but nourishing – perfect late summer fare. Millet is your go-to grain for late summer. A little dairy is fine. And we're coming towards nut season too.

Avoid anything that stresses the spleen, stomach and pancreas – so that's overly sweet fruit juices (tropical mango, papaya, peach), sugar, high-fat foods and food additives.

LATE SUMMER YOGA

Imbalances around the stomach and spleen meridians can lead to feelings of poor self-esteem and of being unsupported, so our yoga practice will aim to bring them gently back to balance.

MULA BHANDA, THE ROOT LOCK

We start by focusing on our root chakra, Muladhara chakra. We're going to practise mula bhanda, the root lock. Yoga recognises three main locks, or engagements. Mula is located in the pelvic bowl, uddiyana is in the diaphragm and jalandhara is in the throat. They are engaged, or held, to help the flow of energy (prana/qi) and to create stability in both our physical and energetic systems.

Find mula bhanda, the root lock, by gently tuning into the area between the anus and the genitals. It's located around the perineum but crucially, above it, deep into the middle of the pelvis. Once mastered it is possible to actually direct energy internally to areas of imbalance and need.

Imagine mula as a central physical location. Play with this, find out what works for you. There's no need to over squeeze or strain – be gentle and simply cultivate a continued awareness of pulling up and pulling in. Aim for a consistency of awareness, so that as your mind naturally drifts, and the lock dissipates because of this, you bring your awareness back to the point and re-engage. Don't worry about the drifting – it will happen a lot until you get used to focusing mind and body together.

Stomach and spleen meridian imbalances are associated with poor concentration and forgetfulness so this kind of meditative practice will really help. You can practise mula bhanda anywhere, any time, in any posture (standing waiting for the bus or sitting watching television). However, don't overdo it. Keep your effort at around the 30 per cent mark and be sure to relax properly between times, or you will set up too much tension in your pelvic girdle. After a while you will notice that it isn't so much about a muscular effort. You will also notice that it's a great way of generating energy.

1. We're going to practise mula bandha in Mountain pose (Tadasana), the most grounding posture in yoga.
- Start by standing with your feet parallel to each other under your hips, pointing directly ahead. Use your second toe as your marker.

- Activate the arches of your feet. It is worth adjusting your feet even a little, if your natural placement is out. The effect will continue up through the body and will have a considerable knock-on effect on your balance. Remember, our feet are our roots and our contact with the earth element.
- Raise your toes and bounce around a little on the balls of your feet then lower the toes and firmly press into the ground with all four corners of each foot.
- Press your knees back slightly and then release so they are soft. Check your pelvis is not tilted too far forward or back – the sacrum usually has around a natural 45-degree angle. You want the natural curvature of the spine, but check if some of your curves have become too exaggerated. You can self-correct using a mirror or consult a postural practitioner or yoga teacher if you are at all unsure.
- Lift the heart area into a gentle back bend on an in breath, and drop your upper body back a little, extending your arms wide. Then, as you breathe out, bring the arms back down to the sides, palms facing the body, fingers pointing at the ground.
- Take a deep grounded belly breath in and bring your chin to your chest on the out breath. Then lift your chin back to a neutral position. Imagine an egg tucked right under your chin, getting the sense of lift through the neck and down into the spine.
- Now tune in to your mula bandha. Spend some time here settling in. Become familiar with all the points of this posture and see if you can foster a sense of complete balance between maintaining your gentle root lock, your physical posture, and your body/mind connection. Breathe into the belly as deeply as is comfortable. Find your centre and stay there. At first it might not be for very long but that's fine – as with all our yoga, this is a work in progress. When you are satisfied that you have progressed

enough, bring your feet together so that they are touching.

2. Now we are going to move from this position into Chair pose (Utkatasana). Inhale deep into the belly and, hinging at the hips, knees and ankles, bend your knees into a downward movement, as if you were sitting on a chair.

- Engage mula bandha and your abdominal muscles. Our focus is particularly on the transverse abdominal muscle – visualise drawing your hip bones towards each other. Engage these muscles first before you lunge.
- Have all your abdominals moving toward your spine. Now place your hands into Prayer pose (Pranamasana), at the level of the heart.
- Take a couple of belly breaths here while you organise yourself and settle into a solid sense of balance.
- On an out breath, gently rotate just your upper body to the left, hooking your right elbow on the outside of the left thigh (if you can – otherwise just gently twist). As you breathe in, come back to centre. On the next exhale, twist to the other side. Once on each side is fine or you can repeat a few times if you like. This posture strengthens the whole system and particularly massages the stomach and spleen areas, aiding detoxification and elimination.

3. Gently come back to standing. We're going to move into Temple (or Goddess) pose (Utkata Konasana) and practise another twist variation.

- Separate your feet wide and bend your knees. Check that your knees are over your heels. Root your feet into the ground and press your thighs back gently. Allow your hips to come down.
- On an inhale, bring your hands palm down on the top of your thighs. With a small push shrug your shoulders up to your ears. You will feel space open up in your spine. Experiment with where

you place your palms on your legs.

- Exhale and twist to the right. Keep your arms long and you can use them as leverage to help you lengthen and twist. Do this gently, being aware of any feelings of strain. Ease up if anything feels pinched or uncomfortable. Remember, we're looking for the edge, not to go over it. Breathe in, come back to centre and on the out breath twist to the other side, shoulders up to ears again. Repeat a few times, as feels good.
- Come back into standing and shake yourself out as loosely as you can.

4. Lie down on your back on your mat ready to come into Bridge pose (Setu Bandha Sarvangasana).

- Bend both knees and place your feet flat on the floor about hip width apart. Your arms lie along the sides of your body, palms facing down.
- Press your feet and arms into the floor and, as you inhale, roll the spine upwards off the floor. Make this move slow and focused, tuning right into each section of your spine. Lift the hips up as high as you can, keeping a sustained lift that also lifts your chest. Breathe and hold for 4–8 belly breaths.
- Roll back down gently, one vertebra at a time, allowing each section of your spine to meet the floor, opening up the spinal processes. Feel free to repeat.

5. To end, we are going to deepen into self-nourishment with a wonderful pose called Legs-up-the-Wall pose (Viparita Karani). It's a lovely way to end your practice, an alternative to Savasana. You will need an open wall space, your mat and maybe a folded blanket or cushions.

- Start seated beside the wall with the side of your body touching it. On an exhale, lie down on your back at the same time as pivoting so the backs of your legs press against the wall. Your feet are facing the ceiling. Shift around so your sitting bones press up against the wall as well. If this isn't available to you, it's fine to have them slightly away until you are more relaxed. If this is at all uncomfortable, use props and cushions. For example, you could press into the wall with your feet and lift your hips to slide a folded blanket under you. You really do need to be comfortable.

- Now let the back of the body be heavy. Your neck should softly relax with your head resting in neutral. Feel the support of the earth along your spine. Your hands can rest on your belly or down by your sides with your palms facing up. Keep your eyes closed, soft in their sockets, and breathe calmly through your nose.
- Stay here for 5–15 minutes. It is deeply restorative and refreshing. To come out of the position, press your heels against the wall, lifting your hips and rolling carefully to one side. Stay on your side for a few minutes to adjust before returning to sitting and then, gently, standing.

MUDRAS

If you prefer to keep your yoga private but would still like to make some power moves while you're out and about, look to mudras.

Mudras are yoga postures for hands and they can influence your body and mind just as much as the full-body asanas. There are mudras to bring about peace and calm; mudras to energise and boost confidence; there are even mudras to help your wishes come true. Simply by bending, crossing or interlacing your fingers – how wonderful is that?

Nobody really knows the origin of these sacred signs. Nearly every ancient civilisation has a variety of hand gestures – some are serene, like the bringing together of hands in prayer, or the outstretching of hands in welcome; some are distinctly the opposite – giving the finger or the two-fingered salute. However, in India and Tibet they have, over thousands of years, been elevated into a spiritual art form.

Ideally you'd practise mudras at a time when you can be quiet and mindful but, you might end up not doing them – so I'll drop into a mudra while I'm on the train or when I'm floating in my bath. Or get into the habit of practising them for a few minutes before you get up or before you fall asleep at night. Settle for one or two at a time, rather than mixing up a whole bunch.

Apana mudra – the energy mudra: This mudra is cleansing as it supports the liver and gall bladder, and helps with the removal of toxins. It also promotes balance, harmony and clear-sightedness. Place your thumb, middle finger and ring finger together (on both hands) and extend your index and little fingers out.

Prana mudra – the life mudra: This is an energising mudra – for when you want to feel more assertive, more confident, and when you need staying power and inner strength. It's wonderful if you're feeling nervous, distracted and jittery. Place the tips of your thumb, ring and little fingers together (on both hands). Stretch out the other fingers.

Kubera mudra – the luck mudra: This mudra is said to help grant wishes, and to help with future plans. Visualise what you need very clearly. Check with your heart that this is not only good for you but also for the world around you. Now press your fingers into the mudra and wish! Place the tip of your thumb, index and middle fingers together (on both hands). Bend the other fingers so they rest in the palm of your hand.

HO'OPONOPONO

Years ago I had a particularly difficult boss and, rather than waste my energy loathing her, I used to blast her with unconditional love. It worked too – after each 'love bomb' she definitely chilled. What was really interesting was that she could tell something was happening. 'Are you doing something weird to me?' she'd say. I'd look innocent and shrug. So, when I learned about the ancient Hawaiian practice of Ho'oponopono, I didn't find it too much of a stretch.

It comes from the Hawaiian verb that means to put to rights, to amend, to tidy up. It's about putting things right not by pushing at external reality but by looking within ourselves. There is an incredible story about a Hawaiian psychologist called Dr Ihaleakala Hew Len who, when he started work at a hospital with the criminally insane, said he didn't need to have consultations with his patients, he just wanted to see their charts. The story goes that he studied the charts and then looked within himself to see how he created each person's illness. As he improved himself, the patients improved. How mind-blowing is that?

Illness, the theory goes, is created by the stress of anger, guilt, recrimination and lack of forgiveness. Not just our own illness, but the wider illnesses of society. So, according to Ho'oponopono, we are responsible for... everything. Yes, even for the terrorists, for the banks and the economy, for pollution and war. So do we have to take responsibility for the haters, for the hitters, for the abusers? Well, why not? Do you know what I've found? It's actually a lot more comfortable to take responsibility than to harbour anger, resentment, sorrow, blame. Who wants to be a victim? Who wants to be eaten up with hate and misery?

In a world that feels like it's spinning further and further into chaos, where it's so easy to feel hopeless, powerless, pointless, maybe this is something small that we can all do. None of us know anything for sure. So why not try?

How do you do it? It comes down to four simple phrases:

I love you.

I'm sorry.

Please forgive me.

Thank you.

It's stupidly simple but I love it. All you do is quietly meditate on a person and just repeat the phrases, throwing out all the unconditional love and hope for forgiveness that you can. It's tough because the mind wants to get caught up in 'yeah but...', and 'but you...' and so on and so forth. Just ignore the mind – it knows nothing. So... I love you. I'm sorry. Please forgive me. Thank you.

FLOWER REMEDY HEALING

There is evidence that many ancient cultures across the world used flowers to treat emotional imbalances. In Europe, the great healer Paracelsus chose essences to treat his patients' emotional traumas. Nowadays, perhaps the best-known flower remedies are those of the British physician Dr Edward Bach who, early in the last century, established his 38 flower remedies based on common trees and plants, such as oak, walnut, and mustard.

However, there are remedies from all around the world – from California, Hawaii and Alaska, from Tibet and the Himalayas, from Australia and the Amazon. One thing they all have in common is their complete safety. Flower essences are the ultimate DIY therapy – gentle, safe healers. However their results can be very profound with the power to heal emotional wounds and transform relationships. So think carefully before you choose your remedy – you could be about to shift your whole life.

I'm going to focus on the Australian Bush flower remedies here, as I have found them to be highly potent healers. Yet follow your heart – you may wish to experiment with essences that come from your own part of the world, or from a culture that interests you.

The essences work, not physically, but on the vibrational level of our feelings and emotions. Generally the flowers are simply put in a bowl of pure spring water and allowed to stand in sunlight for a few hours so that the healing energy of the flowers is transmitted to the water. While everything in life vibrates at a certain frequency, flowers vibrate at a very high level. So, unlike essential oils or herbal remedies, which contain physical substances extracted from plants, there is no physical part of the flower in a flower essence, only its healing vibration. By ingesting the essence, our own emotional vibrations are coaxed into a new, healthier frequency.

However odd it sounds, the remedies do seem to work – and have done for millennia.

KEY ESSENCES FROM THE AUSTRALIAN BUSH

Billy Goat Plum: For anyone who feels repelled by sex, their own body, and sexuality in general. If you loathe your body and feel disgust at its functions, this is a deeply healing remedy. It helps you to accept yourself and enjoy sensuality and sex.

Bottlebrush: For anyone going through a transition in life – puberty, pregnancy, menopause, retirement. It helps when you feel unable to cope with change.

Bush Gardenia: If you've been too caught up in your own life and career to take much notice of your relationship, this remedy might save the day. Bush gardenia helps to reopen channels of communication and puts you back in touch with your partner's life. It's known as the 're-sparker' of relationships.

Dagger Hakea: For feelings of resentment and bitterness towards lovers. Allows forgiveness and open expression of feelings.

Five Corners: A wonderful remedy for lack of confidence and low self-esteem. If you dislike yourself and constantly feel you sabotage yourself and the chance for happiness, try this remedy.

Flannel Flower: A remedy which is particularly useful for men who shy away from relationships because of past hurts and traumas. It helps promote emotional trust, confidence in intimacy and increases sensitivity and feeling.

Gymea Lily: For powerful people who tend to be dominating and demanding, proud and arrogant, used to getting their own way. It reduces the need for status, recognition and being in control.

Isopogon: An ideal remedy for those who feel cut off from their feelings – the type of people who are ruled by their heads, rather than their hearts. It helps you reconnect with your emotions and with forgotten parts of yourself.

Mountain Devil: When you hold grudges and harbour constant suspicion towards your partner. Mountain devil combats ill-founded jealousy and anger.

Peach-flowered Tea Tree: If you can't commit yourself to relationships, or get easily bored with people, try this remedy. It helps those who are easily discouraged and who suffer mood swings. It can balance your emotions and boost your interest in relationships and other projects.

Philotheca: For anyone who has a low opinion of themselves. You may find it hard to accept praise for your talents and successes.

Pink Mulla Mulla: For those who have been hurt in the past and are frightened of being hurt again. This flower helps to release pain from the past and can break down the walls we build around ourselves.

Red Grevillea: For anyone who feels stuck in a rut. You know what you want to do, but not how to go about it. It helps you become more independent and gives courage and dynamic energy to bring about changes you need to make.

Southern Cross: For those who are bitter and resentful, feeling that life has been unfair to them, and that they are hard done by. It helps transform a negative attitude into a positive outlook.

Swamp Banksia: For dynamic, active people who have lost their energy, drive and joie de vivre because of stress, setbacks, overwork, ill-health or trauma. It helps them rekindle their abundant energy and enthusiasm for life.

Wedding Bush: For those who flit from one partner to another, losing interest after the initial attraction. Wedding bush helps to develop commitment and gives the chance of establishing a close relationship.

To make up your own personal blend

1. Take 2 drops of each remedy you have chosen (to a maximum of 5 remedies) and mix them in a 30ml amber dropper bottle (available from pharmacies). Shake vigorously.

2. Fill the bottle almost to the top with spring water and shake again.

3. Now add 1 teaspoon brandy (or cider vinegar) to preserve. Take 4 drops four times daily (either in drinks or neat on the tongue) or as needed.

4. Take the same prescription for about 6–8 weeks, unless another remedy becomes strongly indicated or your circumstances change.

AUTUMN

INTRODUCTION

I always think the shift into autumn is the most easily recognised. One morning you wake up and you simply know that summer has gone. There's not just a nip in the air but a definite change of energy – suddenly everything has an edge, a sharpness, a clarity.

Autumn is a wake-up call to the psyche. It's a dynamic season, one that asks us to kick ourselves into action, to make changes. It's a time to ask questions – about our life path, our true desires. What do you want to do with this one precious life? If that sounds daunting, don't worry. The natural energy of this season might lure you into change without you even being quite aware of what's happening.

Ancient Chinese medicine sees autumn as the time when the energy shifts to that of metal (in Ayurveda it equates to air or vata). It's a real transition time, from activity to rest. Metal energy condenses and contracts, it pulls back and withdraws. It's a time for completing unfinished projects, for gaining clarity. Winter isn't a time to push yourself so

now is the opportunity to bring together all the resources we need to move forwards, into the lean, quiet times of winter.

Metal governs the lungs and the large intestine – both associated with energy exchange and with the elimination of toxins. Our lungs take vital energy from the air and get rid of waste products from our blood. The large intestine takes vital nutrients from our food, while eliminating toxins. However, their role goes beyond the physical. In ancient thought, metal energy is about releasing on an emotional level as well as the physical. It's about letting go of stagnant emotional energy, releasing what no longer feeds our souls. So this is a time for clarity and discernment – for getting rid of everything (whether physical, mental, emotional or spiritual) that no longer serves us. We dump the dross, we clear out.

If we cling sentimentally to old attachments and desires, we may end up feeling melancholy and even anxious. At this transition period of the year, it's quite common to feel the rise of unsettling emotions. Not just anxiety, but also grief and sadness may come to the fore. Rather than ignoring these feelings, sit quietly with them, gently examining them. We'll look at meditation and mindfulness in this section of the book, learning ways to come to peace with our minds and feelings.

The large intestine is also involved with letting go. If this organ has energetic blockages, it can lead to constipation on a physical level, and to hanging onto grudges on an emotional one. Our yoga works with both the lung and large intestine meridians to help release blocks and allow our emotions to run freely.

With our focus on the lungs, we'll look deeper into the fine art of breathing – in the Ayurvedic tradition it's known as 'pranayama' – and it is powerful medicine, both on a physical and an energetic level.

Of course we'll be looking, as always, at how to tweak your diet for optimum wellbeing. It's worth looking into a panchakarma cleanse to clear out all the accumulated yang energy of summer. We'll also plunge into the pleasure of herbs and spices – the ancient medicine chest. The 'evil' of autumn is dryness and it particularly affects the lungs. When combined with cold, it can bring on blocked sinuses and sore throats, so we'll look at ancient cures for these.

On a more esoteric note, we'll dive into the art and science (yes, it really is both) of feng shui, exploring how we can shift our own energy by altering our physical environment. Then we'll end with a treasure trove of crystal delights. It's going to be a great autumn!

AUTUMN DIET

The autumn diet aims to reduce any excess fire energy from summer and prepares the body for the cold of winter. In ancient India and China it was common to start autumn with a gentle cleanse. This is a good time to think about how we nourish ourselves in general.

If you're a lacklustre cook or simply can't be bothered, now is the time to gain incentive. Vata/metal/air energy is soothed and grounded by home cooking, by spending time carefully choosing ingredients and lovingly preparing them. Take your time, develop a routine. You can get away with eating on the hoof during the summer but, come autumn, you need calm, regular, meals.

Base your autumn diet around cooked grains, vegetables and light proteins, which are key to balance in this season. Vata-soothing grains include cooked oats (so porridge rather than overnight soaked cold oats), all forms of rice, amaranth, and ancient forms of wheat. Keep your protein light and easily digestible – meat-eaters should stick to white meat, fish and seafood. Eggs, tofu, nuts and seeds are all good, as are most pulses and beans.

When it comes to fruit, think seasonal. What grows locally? It's tempting to eat imported fruits all year round but your body won't like it too much. In most parts of the world, fruits become less plentiful as we move into autumn. So make the most of the glut of vegetables that come in autumn. Baked pumpkin, stuffed marrows and loaded sweet potatoes are all great autumn dishes – pack them with rice, wild rice, nuts, seeds, and mushrooms (plentiful now) and you'll be thinking the right way. Soups are also great autumn fare and brilliant at using up a fridge full of vegetables. Add in lentils or pulses to make a more solid meal and season with celery and sea vegetables (dulse, kelp, nori) to avoid adding salt.

Go easy on dairy. It always has the tendency to create mucus and that trait is exacerbated at this time of year. If you eat too much heavy cheese and bread, you will end up congesting your body. Other foods that are notorious for creating congestion include cake, biscuits, white flour, sugar and artificial additives (yes, I keep repeating this – at some point it will kick in). The odd brownie or chocolate won't do any harm, but watch out if you're relying on a sugary hit to get you through the day. You will be playing havoc with your blood sugar levels. Far better, if you're flagging, to have a protein-based snack – a handful of nuts maybe, or a couple of oat crackers spread with a pure nut butter.

SPICE IT UP

Ayurveda uses a host of healing herbs and spices to soothe aggravated doshas and restore health. Some should only be prescribed by a physician but there are still many that you can safely use at home. Add them to your cooking or make healing infusions.

Black Pepper: Many Ayurvedic physicians consider black pepper one of the most important spices – it is said to contain all the five elements in equal measure. Add it freely to your cooking.

Cardamom: Promotes digestion and so is often eaten after meals. Cardamom can help indigestion and travel sickness; it also strengthens the teeth and heart. Peal the pods just before you need to use them – crush if necessary. It's a real heart warmer so use liberally – I like to add cardamom to warming drinks.

Cinnamon: Another warming spice that helps to purify the blood and can ease headaches caused by cold weather. It has antiviral, antifungal and antibiotic properties. Add liberally to food and drinks. As a tea, it can help to restore energy, and reduce fever and pain.

Fenugreek: Used in Ayurvedic medicine as a general tonic when you're feeling weak and under par. It's a boon for new mothers who need to increase their production of breast milk.

Garlic: It's a wonderful cure-all. Mash it up and use directly on the skin for wounds; it is also good for insect bites and stings. It is said to strengthen blood vessels and the heart; it promotes good eyesight and boosts the brain and nerves. It is often taken to help prevent arthritis and equally supports the liver and the digestion. Is there anything that garlic can't do? The Ayurvedic sages warned that it is very stimulating so advised stringent meditators to avoid taking it.

Ginger: Buy the fresh root as it is far more effective than the powder. Ginger improves appetite and digestion and is also ideal for soothing sore throats and quelling travel sickness.

Liquorice: Chew the root or take it infused in water as a comforting, invigorating tea. It can help soothe sore throats and ease colds. Liquorice strengthens the eyes and nerves and can help promote good memory. However be cautious if you have high blood pressure.

Turmeric: Is there anyone who hasn't heard about the wonders of turmeric? Ayurveda, of course, has been using it for millennia. If you can, buy your turmeric fresh. It's a potent blood purifier, and is antibiotic and anti-inflammatory in effect, so is useful for wounds and for easing painful joints. It is strengthening and energising – add it freely to your cooking.

AUTUMN YOGA

As we saw in the introduction to this section, autumn is the season of metal, a time to focus on the lungs and large intestine.

1. Sit comfortably on your mat. We're going to start by practicing a particular breathing technique, the Lion's Breath (Simhasana Pranayama). This breath strengthens the face and throat muscles, and improves the voice as it increases blood and qi circulation to the area.

- Release a long exhale and then inhale deeply, directing the breath right to the back of the throat. At the same time, make tight fists of your hands and squeeze up your face. Everywhere in the whole body is squeezed in, as tight as you can manage.
- Release and exhale, sticking your tongue out as far as you can while you make a HHHHAAAA sound (like an angry lion). Look upwards towards Ajna chakra (the third-eye point between your eyebrows) and spread your fingers wide as if they were claws.
- Repeat 4–6 times. Make sure you re-engage your facial and throat muscles each time after your releasing HHHAAAAA breath.

2. From your sitting position come onto all fours for Melting Heart pose (Anahatasana). Make sure your knees are positioned under your hips and walk your hands out in front of you, allowing your heart and chest to sink to the floor.

- Rest your head wherever is most comfortable for you, either to one side, with your forehead resting on the mat, or on a bolster or rolled up blanket. Allow your back to relax and your shoulders to open.
- Stay here, breathing deeply and gently for as long as you feel comfortable. If it feels too strong, use a couple of cushions or a bolster to lie on.
- To come out of the pose, walk your hands slowly back up.

3. Gently come into standing with your feet facing forward. The feet should be 3–4 feet apart with your knees slightly bent to avoid locking the joints.

- Take your arms behind you and interlace your fingers. Keeping your back long, firm up your abdominal muscles and open your heart toward the sky, lengthening your arms downward. Keep the back of your neck long and look up, only tilting the head as far as you can without pinching the back of your neck. This needs to feel comfortable, so don't overstretch. Any pinching at all along

the spine means your supporting abdominal muscles aren't engaged enough, so come out of the pose and re-engage them before continuing.

- Take 2 or 3 deep abdominal breaths.
- On the next exhale, keep your back extended and hinge at the hips into Prasarita Padottanasana, a wide-legged forward bend. Your arms will come up into a vertical position (or as far as is comfortable) with the hands pointing upwards (known as Padottanasana C).
- Stay here for 3 or 4 abdominal breaths (or more if you like).
- On the next exhale come back into an upright stance and release your arms.

4. Turn your feet outwards to a 10 to 2 position. Raise your arms above your head into Prayer pose (Pranamasana), with your arms as close to your ears as is comfortable. This brings the body and mind together.

- Keep your hips steady whilst grounding down through the feet. Lengthening your spine, slowly bend from the waist only, to the left, keeping the hips where they are. Gently increase the space between the hips and ribs, firming up the opposite side. Keep the spine long. Do the same on the right side. Repeat on both sides 2 or 3 times.

5. Now bend your knees and gently drop into Horse pose, also known as Ma Bu or Horse Riding pose (Vatayanasana). This is a transition pose and builds stability. We are borrowing it from the Chinese martial arts as it's a little kinder on the knees. Your feet should be pointing out a little and make sure you can still see your toes as your knees float directly over your feet.

- Lower your knees down to a place that is comfortable yet strongly engaged. Search for a place of comfortable balance – imagine you're sitting on that horse. You do need to feel it but not be in agony.
- Your arms should be level with your shoulders, with your lower arms hinged at the elbows so they point up like an equal-armed cactus with the palms facing inward. (See illustration.)
- Breathe into your lower belly.
- If this feels comfortable, then keep your lower body strong and rooted and gently twist at the waist, turning either way. This helps to tone the diaphragm. Remember to keep your arms aloft to activate the shoulders. Practise this 2 or 3 times on each side, before gently releasing.

6. Now we move into a gentle chest opener. This helps to release any sorrow in a self-compassionate way. It also opens the lungs and eases us into deeper breathing – sadness in particular can tighten and restrict the way we breathe. You can use lots of props for this – no strain involved here, none at all.

- Fold and roll up a blanket. Place it across your mat so it falls just below the level of your armpits. Lie down on your back so your shoulders are gently arched over the blanket and your head is resting comfortably on your mat (use a cushion if it isn't comfortable).
- Now bring your arms back out into a cactus like position (again, you may need cushions or bolsters to make this comfortable).
- Relax here for at least 3 minutes, more if you can. Slow down your breathing, inhaling to the count of 4 and exhaling to the count of 6. When you breathe in, really feel your lungs expand and keep this openness on the exhale. By slowing and deepening your breath, you send a strong signal to your nervous system that you're safe, that it can shift into the parasympathetic system of rest and repair. However, if at any time it feels uncomfortable then relax into your own natural breathing rhythm.

EASING WORRY WITH VISUALISATION

Either stay lying on your mat, moving your body into Corpse pose (Savasana), or bring yourself to a comfortable seated position for a short visualisation. We're going to look at worry – a habit that can become an ongoing concern if we don't learn ways to release it. Autumn is a good time for visualisation practices because we are beginning to turn inwards with the seasonal difference in temperature and light levels, making that natural adjustment towards sleep, dreamtime and the hibernation of winter.

1. Start with a gentle elongation of the out breath, like a deep sigh. Remember that our lung meridian opens into the nose, so this supports the release of built up stagnant energy within the body.
2. As you inhale, imagine yourself breathing in what you need, what supports you in life. A lovely way to do this is to start by visualising something simple like a fresh burst of supporting energy in the form of a soft golden mist.

3. Now, as you exhale, release everything you don't need. Maybe visualise that as a grey cloud, or whatever really expresses what you want to let go. It's your visualisation, so use your own powerful imagination.
4. Continue like this with a curiosity about what comes up for you. It could be something that pops into your mind or, equally, it could be a physical sensation. Breathing in this way can kickstart the release of whatever is no longer resonating with you or truly supporting you.

If at any time you become uncomfortable then stop, rest and let your natural breathing rhythm return. This visualisation helps you become empowered about your own life choices, releasing old feelings that are tying up all your energy, often the cause of exhaustion and depression. Use it to release all these old unprocessed feelings and attitudes that cause anxiety and self-doubt.

PRANAYAMA

Pranayama, the yogic art of good breathing, has been around for more than 5,000 years, while the deep breathing of the Chinese system of qigong is equally venerable.

Science is now accepting that the ancient gurus had it right all along. Research indicates that pranayama can affect a huge range of bodily responses, from cardiovascular activity and hormone balance to shifts in the nervous system.

Breathing is the way we pull in oxygen and circulate it around the body to feed our cells; it is also the way we send out carbon dioxide and waste products, cleaning out each and every cell. However, it's not a case of oxygen equals good and carbon dioxide equals bad. The two gases need to remain in careful balance for optimum health.

The sages didn't just see breathing as a physical act – they saw it on an emotional and energetic level too. Breathing is about taking in new energy and letting go of all that is stagnant. It's about bringing in hope and fresh insights; it's about breathing out all the soul no longer needs. So coughing isn't just about getting rid of mucus and phlegm – on a symbolic level it's about clearing out old emotions and unwanted changes. Notice when you have a cough – what do you really want to get rid of?

Breathing is all about how we tackle life. There is a yoga proverb that says: 'Life is in the breath. Therefore he who only half breathes, half lives.' So breathe deeply and live life to the full.

Our lungs, along with our skin, are the organs that puts us most closely in touch with the world outside – they are the great mediators. Think about this as you try out these simple exercises.

ABDOMINAL BREATHING (BELLY BREATHING)

This is the basic breathing technique taught for general relaxation, stress relief and pain control. It's easiest to learn this method while lying on the floor but, once you've mastered it, you can use it anytime, anywhere. This form of breathing is simply superb for the relief of stress and anxiety. It gives a direct message to our nervous system that we are safe, that it can drop into the relaxed parasympathetic nervous system, switching off our angsty flight/fight/freeze response. If you do nothing else in this book, learn abdominal breathing – everything else will then follow almost by magic.

1. Lie down on the floor. Bring your feet close in to your buttocks and allow the feet to fall apart, bringing the soles of the feet together, with your hands resting gently on your abdomen. If this feels awkward you can place cushions under your knees. This may seem odd but it stretches the lower abdomen, which enhances the breathing process.

2. Breathe in with a slow smooth inhalation through your nostrils, feeling your abdomen expand and contract. Your fingers will part as your abdomen expands.

3. Exhale slowly and steadily through your nostrils, maybe allowing the exhalation to be a little longer, gently blowing outwards. Notice that your abdomen flattens and that your fingers are once again touching.

4. Pause for a second or two and then repeat. Breathe naturally at your own pace in this way for around 5 minutes, or as long as you feel comfortable.

5. If you feel comfortable with this, you can extend the breath so it comes up from the abdomen into the chest as you inhale. This provides a longer, deeper breath.

ALTERNATE NOSTRIL BREATHING

You may be familiar with this technique from yoga. It's a wonderfully soothing breath and can be a real boon if you suffer from insomnia.

1. Sit comfortably in a chair, with both feet on the floor. Be mindful of your posture – imagine there's a string in the centre of your head pulling you gently upright. Allow your eyes to close, your body to relax and your mind to still.

2. Place your dominant hand around your nose. If you are right-handed the most natural way to do this will be to rest your right thumb against your right nostril with the rest of the fingers of your right hand lying gently towards your left nostril. The aim is to close off one nostril at a time, comfortably and easily, without constantly moving your hand.

3. Close the right nostril gently and slowly exhale through your left nostril.

Note that you are starting the breath on an exhale. Then inhale through the same nostril. Pause. Be aware of the pause at the top and bottom of each breath.

4. Swap nostrils by exhaling through the right and inhaling again. Allow your breath to be smooth and relaxed. You don't need to breathe deeply – keep it natural. You may find you need to blow your nose a lot – don't worry, that's perfectly normal.

5. Alternate between the two nostrils for around 5 minutes if you can. If you feel uncomfortable at any time, breathe through your mouth for a while until you can go back to the nose.

6. Once you've got the hang of it, you may like to take it a step further by developing the 'square breath'. So breathe in to the count of 4, hold for 4, exhale for 4, hold for 4. Then take it up to 6 and then to 8.

7. When you're finished, sit and relax with your eyes closed for a while.

TIBETAN RITES

It is said that, for thousands of years, a hidden monastery deep inside Tibet zealously guarded a secret of lasting youth and rejuvenation. The story goes, in the early part of last century, that a frail and elderly retired military officer, named Colonel Bradford, journeyed to Tibet in search of this mythical 'Fountain of Youth'. He found the monastery and was surprised to discover the magical rites were no more than five simple exercises, based mainly on yoga. They were easy to learn and took only a few minutes every day to perform, yet the effects were incredible. When Colonel Bradford returned home, his friends did not recognise him – he looked half his age.

The Five Rites are believed to encourage our chakras to function at their peak, stopping and even reversing the ravages of ageing. It's a lovely idea but, even if we don't all shed decades, they certainly provide the body with a programme of deep but gentle stretching which will help to keep both the spine and its supporting muscles supple, relaxed and flexible. They are also highly energising, stimulating the entire body and encouraging mental clarity.

This series is far more challenging than the yoga we've been doing so far. Start very slowly and gradually build up strength and stamina. If you have back problems or serious health problems, check with a qualified yoga teacher or physiotherapist before embarking on the Five Rites.

THE FIVE RITES

Ideally, perform the rites first thing in the morning. Eventually you should aim to perform each exercise 21 times.

However, to begin with, aim for 10 or 12 repetitions of each move (or even fewer). Make sure you breathe fully during each exercise. Allow yourself a few moments in between each rite. Simply stand quietly, with your hands on your hips and breathe in, through the nose and out through the mouth. Repeat and then move on to the next rite.

Rite #1

Spinning. Simply stand erect with your arms outstretched, horizontal to the floor. Now, spin around until you feel slightly dizzy. Make sure you are spinning clockwise. Before you begin to spin, focus your vision on a single point straight ahead. As you begin to turn, hold your vision on that point for as long as possible and then refocus on the point as soon as possible. Don't be surprised if you can only manage half a dozen spins to begin with – over time you will be able to build up.

Rite #2

Lie on your back (on a comfortable mat) with your palms resting on the floor. Inhale and gently pull your chin towards your chest, point your toes away and lift both legs straight up, keeping your lower back pressed against the floor. Now exhale as you slowly lower your legs and head to the starting position. Rest and then repeat.

Unless you have a very strong core, this will be tough. Try lifting your legs in a bent position to begin with.

Rite #3

Kneel on a mat, with the balls of your feet against the floor and your knees about 10cm apart. Place your hands behind you with the palms resting against the tops of your legs, just below the buttocks. Keep your back straight, and allow your head to drop forward so that your chin is resting against your chest. Now, inhale through the nose and arch your back, pulling your shoulders back, and lifting your head up and back. This will open the chest. Hold for a few seconds and then exhale and return to the starting position. Repeat.

Rite #4

Sit with your legs in front of you, your palms on the floor and your fingers facing forward. Rest your chin against your chest. Inhale, and lift your buttocks and let your head drop back so that, in one smooth move, you've straightened your body from shoulders to knees to make a table. Your feet should be about 15cm apart, your knees bent at right angles and your chest and abdomen parallel to the floor. Your arms are straight. Contract the muscles in your legs, buttocks and abdomen and hold for a few seconds. Exhale, return to the starting position and repeat.

Keep your breathing steady and relaxed through this movement. If you feel out of breath, stop and rest.

Rite #5

Lie face down, and push your torso up so you come into a full Plank pose (Phalakasana) with straight arms (but don't lock your elbows). Both hands and feet should be about shoulder-width apart. Let your buttocks drop so you're almost doing Cobra pose (Bhujangasana) but without your pelvis touching the floor. Look up and ahead. Now inhale and hinge back into Downward-Facing Dog (Adho Mukha Svanasana). Don't lock your elbows or knees – keep them soft. Hold for a few seconds, then exhale and return to Plank/Cobra and repeat. If this is too hard on your back, try a modified version, moving between Plank and Child's pose.

BALANCING BODYWORK

Good bodywork not only feels delicious, it can help to balance your entire system. Massage has clear physiological effects and can ease stress but, as we've already discovered, it can have a potent effect on our emotional wellbeing too.

TUINA

While acupuncture and Chinese Herbal Medicine have become well known around the world, Tuina (pronounced 'twee-nah') is less well known. Yet in Chinese hospitals it is practised equally alongside acupuncture and herbalism as a profound healing therapy.

Tuina is thought to predate acupuncture, providing the Chinese with healing for over 4,000 years. Fundamentally, it is an intense, deep massage that uses a positive barrage of techniques to work on the soft tissue and the joints. It is superlative for treating neck, shoulder and back pain, sciatica, frozen shoulders, tennis elbow and migraines.

It's often used alongside other Chinese modalities. However, it's increasingly available as a stand-alone treatment. Even so, tuina is a deep therapeutic massage – its primary aim is to get you physically well, not to send you to sleep. If you fancy some pampering, this wouldn't be my first choice.

It's not suitable for people with fragile bones and practitioners are cautious when treating those with cancer and heart problems. Certain points are avoided in pregnancy because they could induce labour. As with shiatsu, you do not generally remove your clothes.

TIBETAN MASSAGE

The massage is really only a part of the whole Tibetan treatment, but it is well worth discovering in its own right. The session starts with careful questioning and pulse-taking (as with Chinese medicine, Tibetan healing checks a variety of pulses to gauge health) – expect far more diagnosis than many massages. You might even be asked to provide a sample of urine for diagnosis. The therapist is looking to find out which of the three humours (page 28) – very like the Ayurvedic doshas – are out of balance. This will help him or her decide which oils to use in massage or even whether you need a massage at all.

Pray you do require massage because it is quite lovely. You generally strip down to pants but are well covered with towels at all times and never feel uncomfortable. Practitioners often use oils such as ginger and cardamom and focus on freeing energy blockages via acupressure points. Unlike many massages, Tibetan practitioners will wake you up if you start to doze off – you apparently need to be aware to gain the most benefit.

CHUA-KA

Chua-ka is the ancient Mongolian art of therapeutic massage – purportedly used by Mongolian warriors as a ritual to cleanse their bodies physically and prepare for battle mentally. Apparently, it was also used after battle – to deal with the trauma (both physical and mental) of war. Chua-ka is performed on a couch – you wear just pants but are well covered with towels.

The technique is unusual – long slow fluid strokes which probe deeply into the body. It's been described as 'reflexology for the body' and it certainly feels as if every acupressure point is being targeted in turn. At times it can be almost painful, but the pain is forgotten as your body releases its tension – it's that weird kind of 'good hurt'.

The aim of Chua-ka is to release stored deposits of metabolic waste on the physical level, alongside memories of pain (whether physical, emotional,

mental or spiritual) on the psychological level. Its philosophy reflects that of all Mongolian medicine – treat the whole, not the parts. The belief is that everything that happens to the body is reflected in the mind, and vice versa.

Chua-ka is highly effective for back pain, stress-related problems, and digestive problems. However, most fascinating is the way it seems able to heal psychic wounds. Practitioners say it is ideal for those who are seeking greater self-awareness. I'd agree with that.

MEDITATION

How did meditation begin? It's nice to think our hunter-gatherer ancestors practised while staring at their night-time fires, but nobody really knows. The earliest written evidence comes from the Hindu Vedic scripts, around 1,500 BCE (with practices that dated from 5,000 years earlier or more). By 500 BCE, forms of meditation are also being described in Confucian, Taoist and Buddhist texts in China, India and Tibet.

Originally the aim of meditation was to reach understanding of the higher being (Brahma in Hinduism), often at the expense of the physical body, but Siddhartha Gautama (aka 'the Buddha') shifted the goalposts when he reached enlightenment under the Bodhi tree. After this, Buddhist meditation became focused on realising our connection with all of creation, uncovering what is already here. Zen Buddhism pared the process down even further, just focusing on who we are as an experiential process not dependent on words – so, not conceptualising our experience at all, living in the moment. Many would say that these are all the same thing, and it very much depends on the interpretation and translation of ancient knowledge through the prism and conditioning of whoever is communicating it.

Although meditation is most commonly associated with Hinduism and Buddhism, Christianity, Islam, Judaism and many other faiths have their own forms. The yogis taught that meditation was a powerful tonic and now science is proving them right. Researchers have found that meditation can reduce hypertension, serum cholesterol and blood cortisol, related to stress in the body. It can also mitigate the effects of angina, allergies, chronic headaches, diabetes and bronchial asthma, and help lessen dependence on alcohol and tobacco.

Anxiety, depression and irritability all decrease, while memory improves and reaction times become speedier. One study at UCLA discovered that 20 minutes of daily meditation over eight weeks increased telomeres (the sequences at the end of chromosomes that govern our lifespan), while another found that meditation improves sleep on a par with sleeping pills. Research at Harvard University indicates that regular meditation creates lasting changes in the brain by affecting the regions related to stress, intelligence and wellbeing.

One word of warning – if you have any deep, unprocessed trauma, you may find meditation and mindfulness practices stir it up. If this happens, find a psychotherapist or counsellor to help you.

STYLES OF MEDITATION

Truly, there are a million and one ways to meditate. If you think you can't meditate it's probably because you simply haven't found the type of meditation that suits you. Bear in mind that most ancient forms of practice were designed for male monks living a life of total focus and seclusion. There are some schools of thought that say we modern people need more active forms of meditation. Equally, some say that women's minds are different from men's and so women and men should meditate in different ways. I say just keep trying various types until you find one that rocks your boat and soothes your soul.

Most forms of meditation fall into two main camps (although there is often a fair amount of crossover, and pinning types down is a little like herding cats).

Focused attention meditation: Here your focus is on one particular thing; this could be the breath, a mantra, an external object (candle, crystal, yantra), an interior visualisation or a part of the body. The aim is 'samatha', calming the body and mind. Examples include:

- Metta (loving kindness): a five-stage practice, in which you feel love for yourself, people you love, acquaintances, people you dislike and the whole world.
- Sound or mantra meditation: focusing on a sound or series of sounds. Or, equally, mandala or yantra meditation, where you focus on an image.
- Some forms of Zen meditation where the focus is on the breath, counting, or a 'koan' – a word, phrase or small story that defies being pinned down by the mind alone. The only way to 'solve' it is to embody it totally.
- Pranayama (yogic breathing). Yes, pranayama can be meditation – you're already doing it without realising it.

Open monitoring meditation: In these forms of meditation, your focus is open, allowing yourself to monitor everything that is going on, inside and outside, without judgement or attachment. So instead of pushing away thoughts, feelings, sounds, scents, you would recognise and accept them, without dwelling on them. The aim is clarity and awareness. Examples include:

- Vipassana: also known as 'insight meditation', the aim is to find the truth about our lives via a deep, clear and precise awareness of both mind and body.
- Mindfulness: awareness of being in the moment. We'll go into this overleaf.
- Process-oriented meditation: you work with whatever comes up in the body and mind; it doesn't seek to avoid distractions but to use them for exploration.

SIMPLE WAYS TO MEDITATE

Follow the breath: Start to become aware of your breath – don't try to control it in any way, just notice the inhale, the exhale, and the pause between the two. Every time your mind wanders, gently bring it back to the breath.

Use a mantra: Pick a sound or phrase that appeals to you. OM is the classic (tone it slowly with three sounds – AH-OH-MMM). Or use a vowel sound – such as 'aaah' or 'oooh'. Or pick a word or phrase you like such as 'peace'. Sit calmly and slowly repeat your chosen mantra over and over.

Count to 10 Count very slowly from 1 to 10 in your head, keeping your attention on each number. If you feel your attention wandering (and undoubtedly it will, often before you reach 3!), simply go back to 1 and start again.

Gaze on a candle (trataka): Focus your eyes on the flame and watch it. Notice the way it moves, the colours within it. When your attention wavers or your mind starts jumping, gently bring it back to the flame.

Walk: Walk very slowly, paying attention to every part of every step. Say 'lifting' as you lift up your foot; 'moving' as your foot moves through the air; 'placing' as you place your foot down on the ground; 'shifting' as you shift your weight onto that foot.

Body scan: Scan slowly through your body, paying attention to where you are holding tension. Don't judge or try to let go – just be aware. Move gently from top to bottom, perhaps moving in a spiral around the body, paying attention to any changing sensations.

MINDFULNESS

Mindfulness has been entwined with Buddhism and Hinduism for thousands of years. Scholars claim its roots rightly lie in Hinduism – it's a vital strand in Vedic meditation techniques. However, Buddhism took the concept of mindfulness and... sat with it. Mindfulness (known as 'sati') is considered to be the first step towards enlightenment and it's a crucial part of Buddhist practice. However, mindful practices can also be found in a wide array of other faiths, including Judaism, Christianity and Sufism.

Mindfulness broke free of its religious boundaries in the 1970s. Professor Jon Kabat-Zinn was introduced to meditation by a Zen missionary called Philip Kapleau and went on to study with Thích Nhât Hanh and other teachers. In 1979, he founded the Stress Reduction Clinic at the University of Massachusetts Medical School. Although his Mindfulness-Based Stress Reduction (MBSR) programme used techniques from Buddhism, he made the practice totally secular.

Jon Kabat-Zinn aimed to teach his patients how to kickstart their own healing powers. He found mindfulness could help relieve chronic pain and lessen feelings of anxiety and depression. Patients were even able to clear psoriasis much faster. He went on to instruct people with illnesses ranging from heart disease to ulcerative colitis, from diabetes to cancer.

Since 1970, mindfulness has been scrutinised by a huge number of studies. The results totally support Kabat-Zinn's

beliefs. Mindfulness really can lessen pain and it may also ease insomnia, support weight management, and help reduce depression, anxiety and stress. It is proving helpful in the treatment of addiction and ADHD, and even has benefits for people with psychosis.

Mindfulness can influence our immune system and may even have the potential to influence how our genes express themselves.

Even if there's nothing particularly wrong with you, mindfulness can improve your life, summoning up feelings of joy, peacefulness and happiness. It may even help you discover what you really want from life. However, Kabat-Zinn warns that the very act of stopping and listening can also summon up old suppressed feelings – some people find they need to work through tough emotions such as grief, sadness, anger and fear. So, as with meditation, do find expert support if your feelings become overwhelming or overly distressing.

HOW TO BE MINDFUL : THE BASIC TECHNIQUE

1. Find a comfortable position in which to sit. Create a firm triangular base for your body – you can sit cross-legged on the floor with your bottom on a cushion so your hips tilt forward, keeping your spine straight. Or you can sit upright on a chair with your feet firmly planted on the floor.

2. Make it your intention to sit still but, if you need to move occasionally, that's fine. Don't force anything.

3. You can either shut your eyes or keep your eyes gently focused on the ground in front of you.

4. Slowly bring your awareness to your breathing. Don't try to change it, just watch it. Notice where it is in your body and bring your attention there.

5. Mentally count your breaths. In-breath: 1. Out-breath: 2. And so on, up to 10. Then start again at 1.

6. Thoughts, worries, memories are bound to arise and that's fine. Just notice them. Allow every moment to be exactly as it is.

7. Start small and work up to around 25 minutes.

Does this look very much like meditation? That's because it really is.

THE FOUR FOUNDATIONS OF MINDFULNESS

The Buddha advised working with four foundations in order to train oneself to be mindful.

1. Mindfulness of the body is awareness of the body as a form we inhabit. Here mindfulness exercises focus on the breath. Body awareness may also be taken into movement with walking, yoga, qigong and tai chi.

2. Mindfulness of feelings involves observing bodily sensations and emotions. The key is to let them come and go without judging. They are just feelings.

3. Mindfulness of the mind is known as 'citta', often translated as 'heart-mind'. It is not about everyday thoughts but more about awareness of our mental state (sleepy, anxious, restless).

4. Mindfulness of dharma is also known as the mindfulness of mental objects. Here we practise awareness of how everything inter-exists, how everything is temporary.

BRINGING MINDFULNESS INTO DAILY LIFE

Mindfulness isn't just about sitting in meditation. The ultimate aim is to bring awareness into every moment of the day.

Step by step – *the art of mindful walking*

Yoga and mindfulness teacher Dainei Tracy (the yoga consultant for this book) teaches this technique. It's a lovely exercise for when it's still warm enough outside to walk barefoot.

1. If you can, walk barefoot. Your spine should be straight but not ramrod stiff.

2. Make a loose fist with your left hand and place your right hand gently over the left. Place your hands just in front of your navel area.

3. Drop your gaze slightly, focusing gently on a spot just ahead of you.

4. Lift your left foot slowly. Mindfully and slowly place it on the ground. Feel your heel hit the ground, then the ball of the foot, and finally the toes. Pause, feeling the shift in your weight.

5. Now slowly lift your right foot and repeat.

Raisin meditation – *making every mouthful mindful*

This exercise is particularly useful if you have a tendency to bolt your food. I learned it at The Body Retreat, where they teach mindful eating as part of their weight management routines. It's amazing how your appetite dwindles when you have to give every mouthful this amount of attention.

1. Look at your raisin. What colour is it? How big is it? Notice any ridges or imperfections. Is it dull or shiny? Notice any shadows that fall.

2. Explore its texture. Feel any edges. Is your raisin soft or hard? Can you feel the skin move?

3. Sniff the raisin. Does it smell sweet or dusty? Does it make your mouth water?

4. Now place it in your mouth. Don't chew yet. Notice how it feels on your tongue. Bite into it and notice any sensations. Does it taste different now it's in small pieces?

5. What sounds do you make as you chew? When you're ready, notice your intention to swallow. Imagine the raisin moving down towards your stomach.

FENG SHUI

In the ancient world, great thought was given to the positioning of homes. Buildings were never simply slapped down on any available plot – they were sited according to precise energetic rules. In China, this science of placement was known as feng shui; in India it was called 'vastu shastra'. Although they vary in the details, the major principles are exactly the same.

Feng shui evolved around 5,000 years ago. The ancient Chinese believed that invisible life energy (qi) flowed through everything in life. It's the same philosophy that underlies acupuncture. If it becomes stagnant or blocked, you will most likely fall ill. In acupuncture, needles are used to free any blockages and to regulate the smooth flowing of qi. The principle is much the same in houses and offices – with various 'cures' used instead of needles.

The Chinese believed that the buildings we live and work in require as much attention as our bodies and so developed this complex science for healing our environment. Centuries of observation showed that different areas of the house, office or room attracted specific energies.

Furthermore, they discovered that certain configurations (the layout of rooms or even the position of furniture or features) could either help or hinder the free, smooth flowing of energy. If the energy was blocked or allowed to flow too swiftly it would cause corresponding blockages and problems in life. However,

fortunately, they also realised that small but specific changes ('cures', such as hanging wind chimes or crystals in particular places or using certain colours) could correct such disharmony and put your life back on track. Boosting areas with auspicious colours and objects could even create more balanced energy and better opportunities in life.

Feng shui teaches that by making small shifts to your home you can affect everything in your life – from your finances to your health, from your career to your relationships. It sounds deeply 'woo-woo' but, from my own experience, it works. Partly it's down to psychology – so much of feng shui makes good psychological sense – but there is definitely something else going on. Let's just look at a few ways to spruce up the energy in your space.

- Name your home. Regardless of whether it's one room or a mansion, every home needs a name. Use your intuition to discover what yours wants to be called. You may find it has two names – its formal name and its secret, 'power' name.

- Clear the clutter. Feng shui abhors a mess as it stops qi from flowing freely. Make sure your hallway is clear and welcoming – too many coats blocking the way will limit your opportunities.
- Equally, homes should be clean and well functioning. Everything in the home has a metaphorical meaning – for example, windows are the 'eyes' of the house so if they are dirty you won't be able to see clearly. Make sure your electrics, boiler, cooker and appliances are all working well.
- Choose soft rounded shapes wherever possible. Feng shui sees sharp edges as sending out 'cutting qi' – negative and possibly harmful energy.
- Keep your home full of fresh flowers – they bring a joyous energy into the home. You don't have to spend a fortune on shop-bought ones – bring in some branches in bud or bloom. Give weeds some love.
- Have living things in your home. Animals bring energy into the home, but I appreciate not everyone can share their home with a dog or cat. Goldfish are valued very highly in feng shui – ideally you would have eight red fish and one black in your tank (and keep the water fresh with an aerator – feng shui loves moving water). Healthy plants are great news too – though feng shui prefers plants with soft leaves rather than spiky cacti. Don't try to cheat with plastic or fake flowers – they are not auspicious.
- Sit and lie with a clear view of the door. Beds should ideally be placed in the corner diagonal to the door. Both at home and at work make sure you don't have your back to the door – psychologically it makes you uneasy and energetically it is bad luck.
- Mirrors are known as the 'aspirin' of feng shui as they can reflect good qi and deflect bad qi. However, avoid old tarnished mirrors and keep them out of your bedroom (their energy is too disturbing). If there is no way you can move your desk to have a clear view of the door, place a mirror on it so you can see anyone coming up behind you.
- Wind chimes are a great way to boost an area of your home. Hang chimes by your front door so they gently chime when someone comes in. They can usher in wealth and opportunity.
- Solid heavy things, such as stones, statues and large pots with healthy green plants can be grounding and stabilising. Bring them into your home if your situation is volatile (if a relationship is shaky and argumentative or your job is threatened). Heavy things help you hold on to what you need.

CRYSTAL HEALING

Crystals have been considered to possess healing powers since the dawn of civilisation – witness their use in shamanic ceremonies around the world and their therapeutic use in venerable systems of medicine, such as Ayurveda, TCM and Tibb. If you see a Vedic astrologer in India, it's highly likely you'll be told to wear a particular gemstone or crystal for healing or to bring good fortune.

In ancient Mayan, Aztec and Incan societies, crystals were used to diagnose and heal disease (they were also used for divination). The mythical lost kingdoms of Atlantis and Lemuria were even said to have been powered by crystals. The oldest crystal amulet dates back 30,000 years and is made of Baltic amber.

Rock lovers assert that crystals are the most stable form of matter in the universe, and that their ordered structure can emit consistent frequencies and store tremendous amounts of information (witness the silicon chip in your computer). We're in the realm of vibrational healing – the belief that a strong vibration can bring our own weaker vibrations into balance.

Modern-day crystal healers employ a wide range of methods. You could find yourself lying adorned with various crystals placed around your body. You could be asked to take crystal or gem remedies internally – they're made from the vibrations of crystals, rather than the crude physical form and work in the same way as flower essences. Equally you can make crystal water by placing a (clean) crystal in a jug of water and drinking it through the day. You can even buy bottles with crystal wands in the centre.

Then there's crystal bed healing. Here you lie on a bed with quartz crystals cut to a specific frequency suspended overhead. They are aligned over the major chakras and pulsating coloured light is shone through them. The theory is that, as the colour relating to each chakra is transmitted through the crystal, each chakra is cleansed, and brought into balance with all of the other chakras. You can also, quite simply, wear your crystals. Or pop one in your pocket, under your pillow, on a bedside table or even have a little collection on your desk.

It's easy to roll one's eyes at the idea of crystals having mystical powers but, as I see it, you can't really lose. Even if they do nothing, they look gorgeous and there's no doubt that some just seem to 'call' to you. If you're not feeling the tug of a particular one, this is a good starter list:

Rose quartz: The so-called 'love' stone is as close as a crystal can get to a warm cuddle. It's said to foster positivity and calm, while strengthening any relationship – with others and ourselves. It helps open the heart chakra. Keep one by your bed.

Clear quartz: Known as the 'energy' stone. Quartz amplifies positive energy and dispels negativity. It's a great stone to have close by when you're meditating.

Amethyst: The 'peace' stone. Soothing, and calming, it's another great choice for your bedside table. It's protective and is said to help enhance your psychic abilities. It's believed to cut through illusion and a false sense of ego.

Tourmaline: The 'protector' stone. It's said to boost self-confidence and creativity.

Carnelian: The 'courage' stone. Renowned as a stone of motivation, courage and joy – it's said to balance levels of energy and is strongly protective.

Moonstone: Soft, mysterious and secretive, moonstone protects, calms and encourages. The 'intuition' stone soothes us into living with the natural rhythm of life, plus it's a subtle heart-opener. A highly feminine stone.

Tiger's eye: The 'optimist' stone. It's a stone of balance, self-confidence, strength and courage. It nudges us to try new things, to sharpen our senses and to be the best we can be.

CRYSTAL CLEANSING

Because they are energy attractors, you will need to cleanse your crystals. Certainly cleanse them when you first acquire them and then periodically.

Sun or moon bathing: Leave your crystals outside for a few hours.

Smudging: Waft sacred smoke around your crystals to take away any accumulated negative energy.

Bathing: Providing your crystal is not salt-based (generally the softer ones), you can give your crystals a bath in fresh water with a little rock or sea salt added. Or, place them in a running stream for a few minutes.

SHAMANIC JOURNEYING

Let's move a little further with our shamanic practice, if this is something that calls to you. Journeying is the shamanic way of contacting spirit guides and helper animals. It's a simple yet powerful technique so I'd suggest you only try it if you feel very centred and grounded. If you have any doubts, do go to an introductory workshop held by a practising shaman who will hold the space for you and guides you through the process.

Do not eat before journeying. Find a place in which you feel safe and will not be disturbed. It needs to be warm and comfortable. You may wish to record the instructions – leaving plenty of time in between each instruction. When you become more experienced, you will be able to drum or softly rattle yourself into a light trance state. However, when you're beginning, I'd suggest you use a drumming track (Michael Harner has good ones of various lengths).

Let's start by exploring the lower world.

1. Smudge yourself and each corner of the room you are in (pages 74–75). Put out your smudge stick and make sure it is quite safe (and won't send out sparks) while you are journeying.

2. Lie down on a comfortable mat. It's a good idea to cover yourself with a warm blanket. Some deep abdominal breathing will help you become relaxed. Or maybe move through your body from feet to face, tensing and releasing each part.

3. Just listen to the drumming for a while. Can you feel it in your body? Where? Let your mind follow the drum beats.

4. Bring to mind the intention to find an opening into the earth. It might be a hollow tree, an animal's hole, a cave, a downward sloping tunnel; it might even go through water – a spring or underwater cave. It could be somewhere you have seen recently or somewhere from way back in childhood. Explore the opening. You may want to go as far as this on several occasions before you feel ready to go further.

5. When you feel ready, enter the opening. Everyone's experience is different so don't judge yours. You may tumble downwards, down and down, like Alice in the rabbit hole. You may slide, feeling the sides of the opening. The tunnel may bend. However, it should feel natural and easy. If not, maybe wait until another day.

6. At the end of the tunnel you will emerge in the lower world. Be curious.

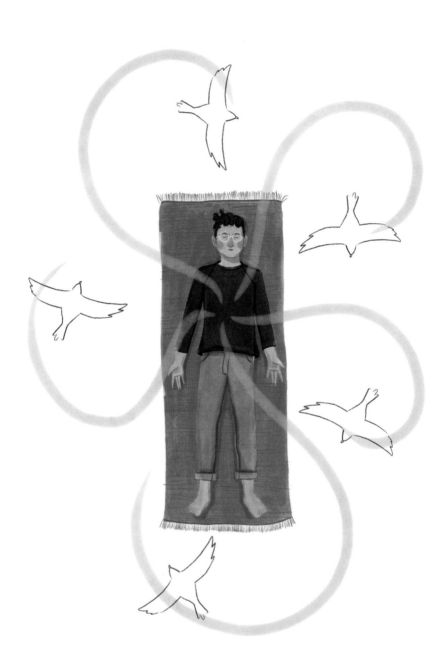

Look around, listen around, feel around. Explore. Again, this may be enough for you. At any time you can travel back, using the drum to ride back to conscious awareness, back through your tunnel.

7. When you're back in the 'real' world, become aware of your body lying on the floor. Wiggle your fingers and toes. Give yourself a good stretch. Get up slowly and stamp your feet on the ground. Have a warm drink and journal your experiences.

FINDING YOUR SPIRIT ANIMAL

Once you feel comfortable using the drum to take you down through your earth opening into the lower world, you can take a journey with the specific aim of contacting your spirit animal, often called a 'power animal' or 'ally'.

Follow the preparations above but, before you start the drumming, set your intention – that you will descend to the lower world and, if it is willing, make contact with your animal (or, more accurately, it will make contact with you).

Now follow the instructions up to the end of step 6. Explore the landscape you find yourself in. The key to finding a power animal is that it will present itself to you four times, in different places or from different angles. Be open to what appears. Drop any expectations of what you think you should have as your animal guide. It could be a mammal or a bird (maybe even a mythical creature). It

might be a snake, another reptile or a fish (but make sure it doesn't have its teeth bared – if so, go back and try again later).

Once you have seen your animal four times, you will need to dance for it. This is seen as an exchange of energy – your gift to the animal which, in turn, will give you your 'power'. At this point pretty much anything can happen. Some animals believe in 'tough love'. You may find yourself 'become' your animal. Or your animal may guide you in some way. Take it slowly. This is a relationship and it should be handled politely and graciously.

You may feel as if your animal is well known to you and it's quite possible it is. Many ancient shamanic traditions taught that as young children we all have spirit animals who keep us safe. The animals only leave if we don't pay them attention. So make sure to honour your animal when you return to waking reality. Dancing is a common way of engaging with your animal (and a lovely one). Take your animal for walks. You may find you take on the skin of the animal and want to run, climb, swim in its guise. Enjoy it!

WINTER

INTRODUCTION

There's a hush, a stillness that descends as we move into winter. Energy condenses and shrinks back, in order to conserve. This is the time of year when many creatures hibernate, so it's no wonder that we human creatures feel the urge to hunker down, to snuggle up by the fire and keep warm, to sleep longer, to dream. We're naturally far more contemplative in the winter months and our energy levels tend to be lower too.

The shorter days mean there is less qi in the air – without the warming energy of the sun. Yet, rather than berate ourselves for feeling sluggish and quiet, let's work with the stillness and embrace the pause of winter. I like to think of it as the season of the soul, a chance to attend to our innermost needs and yearnings, an opportunity to go deep, without the distractions of the busier seasons.

There is beauty in the pristine cold. It's a time to dream, to muse, to divine, to rest. We want to encourage flow at this time while still respecting that this is the season of hibernation and inner focus. Qi can collect and stagnate in the winter more readily, so it's a good time to unwind and reassess the directions to be taken in the forthcoming new year.

In the Chinese system, winter is the season of deep yin energy. It's linked to the element of water, which is considered to be full of hidden potential. Water rules the lymphatic system, our hormones, the bladder and kidneys. It also rules our ears and hearing, our teeth, our sexual organs and our bones, especially the skull and spine. It's a curious list.

We'll be concentrating on the two major winter organs, the bladder and the kidneys. The bladder is thought to be the seat of the emotions in the body, while our kidneys store the energy of the life force itself; they're seen as relating to our entire life cycle – from the great mystery, through our life, to the great mystery again. Willpower is a trait associated with the kidneys and, if you feel as if yours is perilously close to nil, you might well have a water imbalance.

Bladder meridian imbalances can show up as one being fearful, resistant to change – you might be pessimistic and easily triggered. The kidney meridian is also associated with bone marrow, the growth of new blood cells and nourishment. Weak kidneys can lead to immune deficiencies. As winter is the time of chills and flu, it's even more important to focus on the bladder and kidney meridians. Above all, keep them warm and snug (a hot-water bottle swathed in a cosy cover does the job nicely).

In Chinese medicine, the brain and spinal cord are also forms of marrow, so an inability to think clearly and poor memory are signs of deficient kidney energy. The kidneys are the centre of courage, so imbalances also manifest as fear, nervousness and even paranoia (as with bladder imbalance). Our emotional ability to deal with stress falters. Using our willpower and following our own direction can be powerful processes here.

The 'evil' of winter? Unsurprisingly it's that of cold. When our bodies become cold (on a level deeper than just feeling a bit chilly) we can develop headaches, fevers and flu. Cold within the intestinal system can create cramps and pains, diarrhoea and excessive wind.

So, keep warm through these winter months – not just physically, but emotionally warm. This is a time to gather your dearest people around you, in small groups (summer is the big group time) around the fire (even just a tray of candles invokes the warming element of fire), to talk deep, to feel known and hugged and loved.

As you'd imagine, our winter diet is going to be nourishing, nurturing and warming. Our winter yoga practice is strengthening and empowering, working deep into the kidney and bladder meridians.

I'll be encouraging you to nourish your body even further with warming heartfelt bodywork, including some massage techniques you can use yourself (maybe at those home gatherings). We'll indulge ourselves with steam baths and saunas.

Loneliness and depression can rear their heads in winter particularly, so this whole section is about gentle ways of caring deeply for yourself – body, mind, heart and soul. This could involve some gentle dreamworking, or gathering together in soul groups. Finally, we'll delve into the magic of oracles, so we can look ahead to the next year.

WINTER DIET

Our winter diet is predominantly warm and nourishing. We can take robust meals at this time of year, with more oil and fat, but be careful to keep a good balance of carbohydrate, protein and fat so as not to aggravate kapha energy. Equally, you need to avoid very light and cold food, which will upset vata.

Please don't even think about going on a diet during the winter months. It really won't do you any favours. I wince when I see magazines and websites promising you can shed pounds before the holidays. Even worse, I hate the way that New Year now seems to be synonymous with dieting. Please don't do it. You're working against your body and against nature. Yes, you might lose weight but at the cost of leaving your body open to colds in the short term, and deeper imbalances long-term. Wait until spring.

Take your cue from nature – if you eat seasonally and locally sourced food, you won't go far wrong. Root vegetables really come into their own at this time of year – let them form the basis of soups and stews. If you're a meat-eater, follow the ancient European tradition of using just a little meat to add flavour to a hearty stew. Agni, digestive fire, is usually strong during winter so, if you like to eat meat, this is the best time to indulge. Some Ayurvedic physicians also say it's fine to indulge in a glass or two of red wine at this time of year. Ideally drink it before or after your meal, rather than during it.

Get your greens. Again, there are plenty of seasonal options – cabbage, cauliflower, leeks, broccoli and Brussels sprouts are all in season and pack a great nutritional punch. Bulk up everything with onion and garlic, the great purifiers and strengtheners.

Wholegrains and pulses add a further solidity to your food – experiment with the full array of ancient grains and legumes.

Ancient physicians say that the tastes to look out for in winter are predominantly sweet, sour and salty. Just don't let that become an excuse for overdosing on chocolates and crisps!

WINTER YOGA

As we saw in the introduction to this section, winter is all about the kidneys and bladder, so our yoga practice works on these key meridians.

1. Stand in Mountain pose (Tadasana) with your feet nice and square under your hips and your shoulders relaxed (take a moment to check they're not lurking up by your ears). Now tap your thymus – a small gland in the centre of the sternum. In prepuberty it is a producer of white blood cells in the marrow and elsewhere and, while this function lessens with age, it is still a major part of our lymph system and deserves attention.

- With your fingertips, tap firmly all across the centre of the sternum and widen out across the ribcage to include the top part of the kidney meridian, until you can feel a pleasant stimulation and the area is energised.
- Now rub your hands together to create more warmth and place them on the kidneys themselves. Give yourself a gentle rub, calming, self-soothing and warming. Use Ocean Breath (Ujjayi): imagine that you are trying to fog up a mirror in front of you, blowing on it with an open mouth. Now breathe that way but with your mouth closed. The throat constricts ever so gently, like a soft snore or like the sound of the sea, each breath a wave rolling to shore.

It's a soft slow breath, long and relaxed, always through the nose. This pranayama practice builds heat in the body and focuses the mind. It can be both soothing and empowering, as you enter into your own inner ocean.

2. Next, still standing, we are going to practise Laughter Yoga, laughing right into our bones. It's perfect for this time of year as it directly affects our emotional body/the limbic system, which is governed by the kidney and bladder meridians. If your bladder meridian is very unbalanced you may resist this vehemently. It will seem silly and ridiculous. Great – it's a sign you really need it. The body doesn't know the difference between pretend laughter and genuine laughter. The embodiment of joy that this practice creates has many documented benefits (improved immune and lymphatic function, plus re-oxygenation of the blood and cells of the body, all relevant to our kidney and bladder qi).

- To begin, give yourself a big shake. Shake out any tension, just like a dog coming out of water.
- Now raise your hands towards the

ceiling on a big belly inhale and then exhale with a big 'HHHAAA', longer than the inhale. Repeat this a couple of times.

- Next, instead of your 'HHHAAA' sound, laugh on the exhale. Let it all go. 'HO HO HO. HA HA HA.' Just laugh. This may take a bit of practice and it may feel really ludicrous – so, okay, laugh at the sheer insanity of it. Persevere, fake it, just do it. Keep going until you are genuinely laughing – it happens – and then laugh into

your very bones. Close your eyes and feel your skeleton. Laugh, laugh, laugh and bring energy (qi) to your blood cell factories and the marrow. Laugh and let go of anything that you don't need any more.

- When you are finished just stand quietly, hands over kidneys, smiling into your body and all its wonderful processes.

3. Step your right foot back as far as you can into Warrior pose, (Virabhadrasana). Turn the foot inwards so it's at an angle of around 45 degrees. Your front foot will be pointing straight ahead.

- Gently bend your front knee – make sure you can still see the toes of that foot so that the knee is not strained.
- Lift your arms as near to your ears as you can with the palms facing each other and parallel. Breathe into your belly with a sense of grounding through the lower body. Feel each corner of each foot rooting deep into the earth. At the same time feel a sense of lift through your upper body, making space in the hara area. Allow a sense of your own empowerment naturally to arise. Stay for 2–6 breaths.

4. Now lower your arms to shoulder height, palms facing down, and turn your upper body to the right into Warrior II pose (Virabhadrasana II). Your shoulder blades float over the hips and your feet

are grounded. Breathe here for 2–6 deep belly breaths.

- On an inhale, turn the palm of the left hand upwards and bring the arm up and over the head while the upper body arches back towards the (straight) back leg and your right hand slides down that back leg to anchor itself (wherever is comfortable). Look up at your raised arm and breathe here for 2–6 breaths.

- To come out of your Warrior, straighten your legs and lower your arms and then walk or jump back into standing. Repeat steps 3 and 4 on the other side. This is a strong pose that can lessen fear and encourage personal will, so take it at your own pace. Explore.

5.   Next, take yourself to sitting in the middle of your mat to practise Frog pose (Mandukasana). This pose lengthens and stimulates the leg portions of both bladder and kidney meridians. We will practise half Frog with one leg at a time.

- Sitting with your legs straight in front of you, bend your left leg up and then out to the side. Your foot will be pointing backwards and can be either pointed or flexed. If it feels good, bring that foot closer to your buttocks.

- Fold forward over your right straight leg. Explore this. You can widen your leg position and fold forwards as far as feels good. Experiment with the angles of your bent leg – you need to feel an edge while protecting your knee. Can you maybe move a little deeper on the exhale? Hold for as long as is comfortable without strain (breathing all the time – you might manage anywhere from two breaths upwards). Repeat on the other side.

6.   Come into a cross-legged sitting position on your mat with a firm bolster under your sitting bones. The bolster encourages your knees to lengthen away from your hips and supports the lower back in its natural curve allowing the spine to balance without strain.

- Maintain this sense of lift through the back right up to the top of the head. Rub your hands together briskly for 15 seconds, until they feel warm and energised.

- Gently place your hands over your closed eyes, where the bladder meridian starts. Your fingertips rest on your forehead, the palms over your eyes, and the heels of your hands rest on the cheeks. Cup the hands slightly and enjoy how your eyes absorb the soothing darkness, all soft in their sockets.

- Breathe gently and slowly into the belly, your exhales a little longer than the inhales. Continue as long as it feels soothing, up to 5 minutes. Slowly remove your hands and gently open your eyes.

QIGONG

It's said that qigong dates back over 5,000 years, but it could be even older. The story goes that it developed from tribal dances in the Russian Steppes. Smart souls noticed that the people who performed the dances remained supple and healthy. So the dances then travelled, in particular to the Yangtze River Delta where they were formalised into standardised sets of movements.

Qigong combines breathing techniques with mental concentration and precise movements or positions. The beauty of it is that you don't need any level of physical fitness to start – it's exceptionally simple. Some exercises can even be performed in a chair or lying down. Yet don't be deceived – qigong is powerful stuff. The aim is to build up your vital energy, so qigong is often used for a wide range of autoimmune and stress disorders. Let's play with a few simple postures to gain a flavour.

STARTING POSTURE

This most basic of postures will bring you into a deeper awareness of your entire body. It is grounding and profoundly soothing for the mind. Best of all, you can do this anywhere – I practise when I'm waiting for a bus or queuing at the supermarket.

1. Stand with your feet shoulder-width apart. Keep your body relaxed and experiment to find where you feel naturally comfortable and balanced.

2. Bring your attention to each part of your foot – to the sides, to your heel, your little toe and big toe. Keep all your toes relaxed and in touch with the ground.

3. Bring awareness to your knees – check that they are exactly over your feet and that they are soft and relaxed.

4. Release your lower back; pay special attention to your stomach and buttocks. We hold so much tension in our bellies and our buttocks. Bring awareness there.

5. Now let your chest become hollow. Let your shoulders drop and allow them to become slightly rounded.

6. Imagine you have a string that

stretches from the very top of your head to a rafter on the ceiling. Feel your head float lightly and freely. Let go of any tension in your tongue, mouth and jaw. This is another area in which we hang onto stress.

7. Stay here with your hands hanging loosely by your sides for a few minutes.

8. You can leave it at that or, if you like, take it one step further by visualising the five elements. Start with the earth element – feel yourself grounded, weighted, as if you were a tree with roots stretching deep down into the earth.

9. Now focus on water. Feel a sense of looseness and fluidity in your body. Bring your awareness to the movement of blood and lymph within you – the swift stream of blood; the slow flow of lymph.

10. Air ushers in a sense of lightness and transparency. Pay attention to your breathing, to the inhale and the exhale. How does your breath change as it comes in and out of your body?

11. Now focus on fire – feel its warmth, its energy, its sparkle and unpredictability. Become aware of your heart, its loyal steady beat. Can you visualise the spark of vital energy that tingles through your body?

12. Finally think about space – think about the spaces within your body – the gaps between your joints, your muscles, your cells. The synapses. Bring your attention to the pause between the inhale and exhale of each breath.

SUPPORTING THE SKY

I love this exercise because it really supports the lungs. The best time to perform it is first thing in the morning – it helps empty the lungs after sleep. It is also said to ease backache.

1. Stand in the starting posture (page 169).

2. Hold your hands in front of the energy centre known as the 'lower dantian', just under your navel in the area of the belly. Have your palms facing up and your fingers pointing to each other.

3. Slowly raise your hands up the front of your body and, as your hands reach your chest area, turn your palms so they face your torso. Breathe in. Keep your back straight but relaxed. When your hands become level with your face, roll them over so the palms face upwards. Stretch your arms up over your head and look upwards. Don't strain – just stretch as far as feels comfortable.

4. Open your arms out to the sides. Softly lower them down at the same time as you gently bend your knees. Keep your back straight until your hands are back where they started. Breathe out as you come into this position. Repeat at least 5–6 times for the best benefit.

NOURISHING BODYWORK

There's no bad time to have massage. Yet, even if you don't usually bother with bodywork, make time for it in winter. Our bodies really relish warmth and nurturing touch at this time. One of the most luxurious treatments of all is Ayurvedic 'abhyanga'.

AYURVEDIC ABHYANGA

Ayurveda is massage royalty, with a host of healing treatments that are as delicious as they are efficacious. If you possibly can, hunt out the genuine article and treat yourself. However, if you don't have an Ayurvedic clinic on your doorstep, you can certainly get good results with a DIY version. You don't need to be an expert – just willing.

Abhyanga is a deeply relaxing massage that soothes the nervous system. It also stimulates the release of impurities from the cells and improves circulation to the subcutaneous tissues. Traditionally, it's performed by two therapists working in perfect synchronisation (massage bliss), but you will still get a good result with just one pair of hands.

Be warned, this is a messy massage, so use old sheets and towels. Ideally you should be totally naked for this but, if you feel uncomfortable, wear an old pair of pants, or a muslin loin cloth.

1. Warm the oil to body temperature (the easiest way is to use a bain-marie – placing the bowl of oil in a larger bowl of hot water). If you're massaging a vata type of person, use sesame oil. For pitta, choose coconut (unless it's very cold, in which case, stick to sesame). Use less oil on kapha – either sesame or mustard oil is ideal.

2. Place a warmed towel on the floor. Have your subject lie on his or her front to start.

3. The abhyanga touch is repetitive and rhythmic. It should be very gentle for vata, a little firmer for pitta, and can be quite strong for kapha (don't prod and press – the massage must always flow).

4. Use circular movements over rounded areas such as shoulders, hips, scalp, and long straight strokes over straight areas such as legs, arms and neck.

5. Start by massaging the oil gently and smoothly into the scalp and neck. Then continue down the back onto the hips and buttocks. So many massages ignore the buttocks yet they hold a lot of tension.

6. Work down each leg in turn and give the feet and ankles particular attention (the feet can take firmer pressure). Massage between each toe.

7. Now move back to the shoulders and work down each arm. Remember to use circular movements over the elbows and wrists. Massage each finger.

8. Ask your subject to turn over and massage the arms, legs and chest. Traditionally the breasts are also massaged, but check your subject is comfortable with that. Massage the abdomen with soft circular strokes.

9. Now cover your subject with towels or a sheet and move to their neck and face. Use tiny gentle movements over every part of the face. Very gently work inside each nostril. Give each ear lobe a firm tug and massage very gently inside the ear (don't poke or prod). Keep your fingers on the first ridge of the ear.

10. End by gently massaging the third-eye area (just above and in between the eyebrows) with your thumb. Use tiny circular movements and spend at least 5 minutes here.

11. Make sure your subject is warm and comfortable. They should rest and relax for between 15–30 minutes.

BATHING

Nothing beats a hot bath when it's cold and miserable outside. The ancient Egyptians, Babylonians, Greeks and Romans all extolled the virtues of a long soak – and therapeutic bathing is still revered in many cultures (from Russia's banya to Japan's furo and sento, not forgetting the wonders of the Arabic hammam).

A good bath can help banish stress, soothe insomnia and relieve aches and pains. It can improve cardiovascular health and it can even help reduce blood sugar levels in diabetics – the heat dilates blood vessels, improving blood flow and helping the body make better use of insulin. The tub has even been shown to ease loneliness – the warm water acts as a watery alternative to a gentle hug. Let's focus on the comforting aspects of bathing.

For stress reduction: Soaking in warm water daily has been shown to be better at easing anxiety and stress than a prescription drug. The key here is to avoid a very hot bath – aim for warm or neutral (body temperature) for the best stress reduction. Essential oils can boost the stress reducing effect – the most effective include lavender, rose, geranium and bergamot.

For detoxing: The skin is the largest organ for elimination and simply by soaking in a long hot bath you can encourage the removal of toxins through the skin (the heat opens up your pores and helps you perspire, as you would in a sauna or steam room). The ideal temperature for detoxing is 32–35°C (90–95°F). Soak for a minimum of 10 minutes (preferably more). Adding Epsom salts to a bath can increase the detox effect but be careful if you have high blood pressure.

For insomnia: Having a warm bath just before bedtime temporarily raises your body temperature and then, as you get out of the bath, it lowers, telling the body to produce melatonin, which induces sleep. The warm water also soothes muscle tension. Use either a long hot bath or a shorter, 15–minute neutral (body temperature) bath. Essential oils can increase the soporific effects, having a marked effect on sleep and its quality – try lavender, sweet basil and jasmine. Research has found that jasmine essential oil has a direct effect on a brain chemical called GABA, helping to soothe anxiety and encourage good sleep.

For skin healing: Keep the water temperature warm. Oatmeal is a supremely soothing addition as oats contain up to 20 times more silica in them than other plants. Silica helps to strengthen the skin and gives it elasticity and smoothness. The active extract in oats, *Avena sativa*, has been shown to help reduce skin irritation and inflammation – conditions such as eczema, dermatitis, psoriasis, shingles and impetigo all benefit. Dead Sea salts also have remarkable skin-soothing properties while home store cupboard cures include cider vinegar, baking soda (sodium bicarbonate) and the juice of the aloe vera plant.

For aches and pains: Whether you ache from a tough workout or from joint problems, a deep hot bath can be helpful. If you can face it, alternating hot and cold baths (or showers) can make a difference. However, for now, keep to warm – experiment with the level of heat, so you don't cause yourself more pain. Epsom salts (made from the mineral magnesium sulphate) help to sedate the nervous system and relax muscles.

Caution: Do not use heat on a fresh injury as it can increase blood flow and inflammation and cause tissue swelling.

For libido-raising: A long indulgent soak is perfect for indulging the senses and switching on one's sensuality. Keep the water pleasantly warm, rather than piping hot. Certain essential oils directly affect the brain, putting you in the mood for romance. Ylang-ylang is renowned as an aphrodisiac – it shouts out sensuality and is also supremely relaxing and anxiety-soothing. Sandalwood and patchouli are two other super-sexy oils, used for millennia to arouse desire.

For emotional healing: It's not just physical; a warm bath has a proven effect on improving mood and emotional well-being. The water really does comfort and soothe – who knows, maybe it takes us back to the womb. Make your bath-time a regular soothing night-time ritual, using candles and warm towels alongside bath unguents (over time your mind will come to recognise bath-time as a prompt to relax and feel good).

Note: When it comes to bath potions and unguents, keep it natural. It usually takes chemicals to get baths foaming and frothing and you don't want to absorb nasties through your skin. The products I keep coming back to are ila and ilapothecary, Aromatherapy Associates, Neal's Yard Remedies and Weleda.

STEAMING AND SAUNA

The ancients knew a thing or two about heat. The rejuvenating effects of wet and dry heat bathing were known to the Romans, the Aztecs, the Native Americans, the Africans, the Russians, the Turks, the Indians (and on and on). The Finns have been promoting the powers of sauna for over 2,000 years and to live without sauna is unimaginable. Ninety-nine per cent of Finns take a sauna at least once a week. For them, it isn't just about physical hygiene and health, it's as much social and psychological.

Sauna is a huge leveller – without clothes (sauna in Finland is always naked), you have no idea what people 'do' – you don't judge them by their position, their affluence, their style. When I was on retreat in Finland, I finally got over my fear of naked sauna. There is something about being physically bare that makes one feel free to bare oneself emotionally too. We talked honestly; we confessed to tough stuff; we laughed like drains.

Once you got sufficiently sweaty, you'd stand up and shower yourself with cool water. There were brushes for scrubbing and also bundles of birch twigs and leaves, known as 'vasta', for gently whipping your body. It sounds masochistic but it feels great – and by stimulating the circulation, makes your skin super soft.

In Finland, sauna is used to treat rheumatism, to ease allergies, to banish colds and to boost poor circulation. It's popular amongst athletes post-workout. During a 15–20 minutes sauna or steam, your body temperature rises, speeding

up the rate of chemical reactions in the body. However, as with all things, exercise caution if you have health issues (in particular cardiovascular conditions) or are on prescription drugs. Sauna is not advised during pregnancy. Also, however tempting it is to 'sweat out' a hangover, you shouldn't use a sauna in conjunction with alcohol.

If you can't get to a sauna, you can try it at home by immersing yourself in a bathtub of hot water, gradually making the water hotter and hotter. While you're soaking, sip a sweat-inducing tea (ginger is ideal). You can make up a brew in a thermos so it stays warm. Soak for 15–20 minutes. When you're cooked, get out, dry off and wrap yourself in a thick layer of blankets for at least half an hour.

DREAMWORKING

Most ancient cultures took dreams very seriously. In ancient Greece it was common to spend time sleeping in a sleep temple – an asklepion – in the hopes of receiving a healing dream. Years ago, I was lucky enough to go on a dream healing pilgrimage through the Greek Peloponnese, visiting and meditating at ancient dream healing temples. I was even more lucky to receive a therapeutic dream while lying on the ancient stones.

The Greeks don't have the monopoly on dreamwork. The Egyptians also had dream beds in some of their temples. They believed the gods would show themselves through dreams and the 'Dream Book', which dates back to the reign of Rameses II, lists dreams and interpretations, dividing dreams into auspicious and non-auspicious. Ancient Babylon was big on dreams, and even the Bible includes many examples of prophetic dreams. Dreaming is equally considered a form of healing in Native American, African, Aboriginal and Torres Straits Islander cultures, to name but a few.

It's a huge subject and I can barely touch the tip of it here but, suffice to say, paying attention to your dreams can only enhance your life in so very many ways.

Dreams can be a passport to a renewed sense of creativity, a fresh way of working out tricky problems and relationships, a means of realising your deepest desires and coming to terms with your deepest fears. They can even alert you to health issues.

Some psychotherapists (particularly those working in the Jungian tradition) say that a dream is our unconscious talking directly to us – it's a direct route to the psyche. Interestingly, it is not only emotional or mental relief that can come from working with dreams. Often quite physical symptoms can vanish. This can be powerful and sometimes painful work and you might feel more comfortable working with a trained therapist if difficult emotions or memories start to emerge.

RECALLING YOUR DREAMS

Some people insist they never dream yet, really, it's more a case that they don't remember their dreams. There is no one infallible way to remember dreams but these few tips might be helpful:

- Simply make an intention to remember your dreams. Our subconscious is always listening and simple intent can be surprisingly effective.

- Keep a notebook or recording device by your bed (ideally not your phone) so that, the moment you wake from a dream, you can jot it down or speak it out.

- If you really never remember dreams, try setting a (gentle) alarm to wake you around 90 minutes after you usually fall asleep. Most dreams happen in REM sleep towards the end of each of our 90-minute sleep cycles.

WORKING WITH DREAMS

Often, simply writing down your dream can bring insights. However, these techniques can help you work further with your dreams.

- Place two cushions facing each other. Sit down on one and imagine your dream character on the other. Tell the character how you felt and ask it a question. Maybe you were frightened by it, or puzzled by its words or actions. Then switch places and imagine you are the dream character – answer the questions. You may be surprised at what comes up.

- Draw or paint a powerful dream. It doesn't need to be 'good art'. You can either paint a scene or simply use colour and shape to express the mood of the dream. What do you notice when you see it expressed on paper? Try turning the picture on its head or side – sometimes other things will pop into your head.

- 'Dream the dream on.' Breathe deeply to relax yourself. Now take yourself back into the dream. Let your imagination run free to imagine what might happen next.

DREAM SYMBOLISM

Our dreams are very much our own and there's little point turning to the dream dictionaries that abound online. It is much more revealing to ask what any particular symbol means to you. Another tip is to focus on the feeling of the dream. Did it make you happy, sad, anxious, exhausted? Having said that, there are some universal archetypal meanings that seem to run through our dreams.

A house: A house usually represents the self, with the rooms symbolising various aspects of our personalities. So, the cellar tends to represent the unconscious mind, while the attic relates to our spiritual aspirations. A dilapidated house can indicate health issues or severe stress. A house on fire can suggest inflammation in the body. New rooms in an otherwise familiar house may mean you have unexplored talents or opportunities. Scary parts of a house may indicate areas of your life you are nervous about exploring.

A journey: Dreams about journeys are metaphors for our journey through life. Difficult journeys show how our own attitudes make life tough going. What form of transport do you use? A train may indicate passivity or lack of choice. Planes may suggest you want to travel far and fast. A plane that never gains height could indicate you are finding it hard to move forwards with a project.

Anxiety dreams: Recurring anxiety dreams indicate you have unfinished emotional business that needs resolving. Being naked in a public place could mean you feel vulnerable in some area of your life. Being lost suggests you may need to shift your life in some way – be it your career, relationship, lifestyle. Being chased usually hints at something you are trying to avoid – if you turn around to confront your pursuer you may find that he, she or it represents unresolved issues or underused abilities. And those disturbing 'going to the loo' dreams? All about our creativity, apparently.

ORACLES

Oracles are part and parcel of the ancient mindset. Originally an oracle was an actual person, usually a priestess, who was considered a portal to the gods (much in the way we might think of a medium as a portal to the dead).

Ancient Greece had many famous oracles, based in Delphi, Epirus, Corinth, Bassae, Delos, and Aegina, to name a few. However, ancient Assyria and Egypt weren't short on oracular wisdom either. In ancient India an oracle was known as 'akashwani' (meaning an unseen person) or 'asariri' (the voice from the air) and India still has living oracles. Hawaii also had oracles at certain of its heiau (temples), and oracles have been part of many ancient African cultures, including those of the Igbo and Yoruba peoples, as well as parts of South American traditions.

Aside from these embodied oracles are the great systems of divination which also stretch across the ancient globe. China gives us the I Ching, the Book of Changes. The Norse tradition bestows the runes. Meanwhile the origins of the tarot really are lost in the mists of time, although it seems likely they originated in Egypt before coming to Europe in the late fourteenth century.

Right now we're seeing a huge upsurge of interest in divination and new oracle packs and tarot decks are springing up all over the place. Nowadays, the focus is not so much on predicting the future but on using the subconscious to foster self-development, to inspire personal change.

For serious practical advice I turn to the I Ching. It predates acupuncture and is the foundation upon which all elements of Chinese philosophy and science are based. Just as acupuncture clears away blockages in the body, by allowing qi to flow freely, so the I Ching advises you on how to move freely and easily through life itself – you literally move with the flow. It was taken very seriously by Chinese rulers as it can be strategic, pragmatic and political.

Bottom line, it's a personal guidebook on how to handle the complexities of life and will give you precise instructions on how to deal with everything – your career, your relationships, your family, your health. If you're remotely dithery, it's also a great decision-maker. How do the I Ching, and all these oracles, work? Most likely, they're connecting us to the intuitive side of our brain, acting as a bridge between our unconscious wisdom and our cognitive brain.

With so much choice out there, which system do you choose? I'd say let your intuition guide you and you won't go far wrong. Browse the packs online or in New Age shops and odds are one will jump out. If not, then I'd suggest you start with the Rider Waite deck for tarot. The Osho Zen Tarot is a modern take that is great for inspiration and creativity. Life coach Kate Taylor has produced a fabulous oracle deck called Practical Magic that just oozes vibrancy and gives little tasks to perform to jumpstart your day.

If you really want to tap into your own ancient wisdom then why not make your own pack of cards, using paintings, favourite quotations, collage, photographs? It's a perfect craft for the dark days of winter.

END THOUGHTS

Now we've come to the end of this book. It feels a little sad, as all partings tend to feel. I sincerely hope you have learned a little, felt inspired a little, been moved a little to try some ancient wisdom. Bear in mind this book is only a taster, a starting point, an introduction. If you want to dive deeper into the various forms of ancient wisdom there are many wonderful resources out there.

I often share my latest findings on my social media pages. I'm *@exmoorjane* on Instagram, Twitter and Pinterest, and *eJaneAlexander* on Facebook. Do pop by and say hello – and share any of your own favourite forms of ancient wisdom.

RESOURCES

Inspiring people and places mentioned in *Ancient Wisdom for Modern Living*

Dainei Tracy: *greatpeace.co.uk*

Jay Griffiths: *jaygriffiths.com*

Viva Mayr: *vivamayr.com*

Michael Harner: *shamanism.org*

Sobonfu Somé: *sobonfu.com*

Donna Lancaster: *thebridgeretreat.com*

Adele Nozedar: *adelenozedar.com*

Fiona Arrigo: *aplacetoheal.co.uk*

Karen Kingston: *spaceclearing.com*

Denise Linn: *deniselinn.com*

Arnold Mindell: *aamindell.net*

Jamie Sams: *jamiesamsbooks.com*

ilapothecary: *ilapothecary.com*

Eleanor's Byre: *eleanorsbyre.co.uk*

Jonathan Goldman: *healingsounds.com*

Soul Medicine: *soulmedicine.me*

Wah!: *wahmusic.com*

Deva Premal: *devapremalmiten.com*

Sandor Katz: *wildfermentation.com*

Moinhos Velhos: *moinhos-velhos.com*

Jan Day: *janday.com*

Edward O. Wilson: *eowilsonfoundation.org*

Kate Roddick: *kateroddick.com*

Gomde: *gomde.org.uk* (plus centres around the world)

Jon Kabat-Zinn: *mindfulnesscds.com*

Thich Nhat Hanh: *plumvillage.org*

The Body Retreat: *thebodyretreat.co.uk*

Kim Bennett: *serenityretreat.co.uk*

Sue Weston: *sueweston.com*

ila spa: *ila-spa.com*

Aromatherapy Associates: *aromatherapyassociates.com*

Neal's Yard Remedies: *nealsyardremedies.com*

Weleda: *weleda.com*

Tsultrim Allione: *taramandala.org*

Kate Taylor: *katetaylor.co.uk*

INDEX

ACKNOWLEDGEMENTS

I have had the honour to learn from so many wisdom keepers over the years. Deep gratitude to them all, including Kate Roddick, Fiona Arrigo, Denise Leicester, Donna Lancaster, Gabi Krüger, Kim Bennett, Gertrud Keazor, Adele Nozedar, Zena Hallam, Caroline Shola Arewa, Amisha Ghadiali, Jane Mayers, Will Parfitt, Jan Day, Doja Purkit, Susan Lever, Jill Purce, Kenneth Wingrove-Gibbons, Benny Mei, Karen Kingston, Denise Linn, Sarah Shurety, William Spear, Jessica Loeb, Rosalie Samet, Maria Mercati, Malcolm Kirsch, Sue Weston, Dr Rajendra Sharma, Andrew Johnson, Dr Natsagdorj, Dr Mohammad Salim Khan, Sebastian Pole, Leo Rutherford, Sara Hooley, Margot Gordon, Ramses Seleem, Paresh Rink, Faraaz Tanveer, William Bloom, Mangalo Upasaka, Juls Abernethy, Simon Buxton, Tuulia Syvänen, Kate Taylor, and Gail Love Schock, to name but a few.

Dainei Tracy not only gave her wisdom as yoga consultant for this book but kept me grounded throughout the writing process – I'm blessed to know her. Adrian Tierney-Jones acted as an early sounding board – thank you.

I'm very lucky to have Kyle Books as my publishers. Deep thanks to Jo Copestick who set the ball rolling and to Sophie Allen who is a dream editor. Maggie Cole brought my words to life with her delicious illustrations, while Sarah Kyle, Cathy McKinnon, Caroline Alberti, Annie Wilson and Becci Woods did the tough behind the scenes stuff that goes into creating the book you hold in your hands. Thank you all.